Thre Cups of Tea

MW00938966

and

The Toughest Job You'll Ever Love

*Riding the Peace Corps Rollercoaster
in Mali, West Africa*

Asifa Kanji and David Drury

D. Drury & Sons, Publishers
London + Berkeley + Hilo + Ashland

This is our personal story. The views expressed in this book are the authors' alone, and do not reflect the official positions of the U.S. Government, Peace Corps, or the Malian Government.

Except in the case of well-known public figures, all Malian personal names in this book are fictitious.

The slogan 'The Toughest Job You'll Ever Love' was created for Peace Corps in 1978 by the advertising agency Ted Bates & Co.

Proceeds from the sale of this book will be donated to the Peace Corps Partnership Program (PCPP) to fund volunteer-led grassroots projects in Mali.

Inquiries and comments may be sent to:
ddruryandsonspub@gmail.com

ISBN-13: 978-1508638469
ISBN-10: 1508638462

To mum and dad, my greatest teachers, with love and gratitude.
Your spirits live on.

There are no foreign lands.
It is the traveler only who is foreign.

-Robert Louis Stevenson

Map of Southern Mali

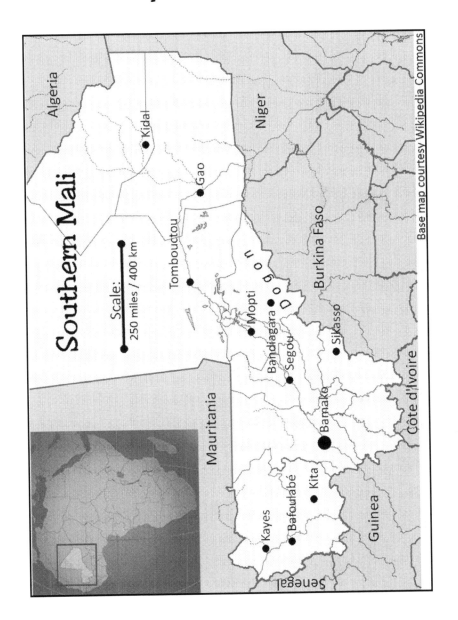

Contents

Three Hundred Cups of Tea - Asifa Kanji

Contents

Contents

The Toughest Job You'll ever Love - David Drury

Contents

Contents

Acknowledgments

We would have no story to tell if it were not for a universe of people challenging us, babying and encouraging us in so many different ways. When we jumped, they all gave us courage, hope, support and the wings to fly.

Heartfelt gratitude goes to the people of Mali, who let us into their lives with open arms and considered us a part of the family.

Special thanks to Mike, Jolie, and all the awesome Peace Corps Mali staff who supported us and our projects; and to the Language and Cultural Facilitators, who helped with our training and did what they could to hammer Bambara into our aging brains.

To the Kayes*kaw*, the Kennedys and to all the Mali volunteers; to our PC Volunteer Trainers, and our missionary friends: we could not have hand-picked a better set of folks to work alongside.

This book started as a series of monthly epistles to the many friends and family who supported our adventure and service with e-mails, care packages and tons of moral support. It was you who pushed us to publish our story. Here it is – this is for you.

Two people who deserve very special thanks are Diane Kimball and Kendal Lyon. Your feedback on our manuscript was above and beyond the call of duty and friendship. Thanks from the bottom of our hearts for all your help in shaping this book to what it is.

-Asifa and David

Three Hundred Cups of Tea

Asifa Kanji

The Prequel

"Big changes are in store for us over this next year," I wrote in my 2009 year-end letter, but who knows what I was thinking back then. I had no idea then that my mother would die, that I would become an American citizen, and I'd find myself on the plane to Africa to serve in the Peace Corps, throwing me into the jaws of hunger season, into the loving arms of families I didn't even know I had and, rather prematurely and undeservedly, into the burning heat of hell.

My mum was a museum of diseases – cancer, lupus, rheumatoid arthritis, and an enlarged heart. Each time her heart, chest and feet swelled up, the ambulance scurried her off to her 'four star hotel.' Medics would pump out the liquid, giving her a new shorter and weaker lease on life. Hearing that she's been admitted would have me jumping around like a fly being chased by a swatter. Frenetically I would get my immediate life in order, catch the first flight to London, and stay for a month, or two, or three, depending on how she was doing. As I would leave to return to Hawaii, I would watch her tiny frail figure framed in the paned window, her white hair blending with her white nightie, so alone, so vulnerable, a ghostly apparition waving, trying to catch that one last glimpse of me. Would this be my last image of her? Was I abandoning my mum? Stifling the tears, and swallowing that lump, I would ask the cabbie about his mom and wife and kids.

"Didn't go out today," she told me on one of our nightly calls.

"Why?"

"Just didn't feel like it."

1

Was she was having another episode where her feet and lungs were beginning to fill with fluid, signaling heart failure? No way was she going to tell me her symptoms, if only to keep me from jumping on the next flight. Umpteen phone calls later, to neighbors, caregivers and close friends of hers, my suspicions were confirmed. Of course I took the next plane out, but this time, in my heart I had already decided to stay with her until her last breath, no matter how long that was. It was just a month.

In her last days, twenty to thirty visitors stopped by every day to see her. The nurses suggested putting up a 'no visitors' sign to allow her some rest. She refused, saying she had all eternity to sleep. She continued to welcome and bless each of her visiting friends, giving each one all she could with her ebbing energy. It was the hole in her heart that rattled death's door, and death took her away ever so quietly.

Embedded in my soul is the tape of my mother's voice: "You must do for others; it is the only purpose in life God accepts." She certainly taught herself well, as doing for others was what she did relentlessly, whether they wanted to have anything done for them or not – the daughter's perspective!

Is it an empty nest when parents die? My mother had just passed away and my father had died nineteen years earlier, not long after his sixtieth birthday. At 57 I was left with, *What do I now do with my life?* Too young to retire, too old to start again... or was I?

"Be of service to others," my mother chimed in.

She does that all the time, barging in when I least want her opinion, as though she were living in my head. Well if I had my choice, I would run away and join the circus or walk from Cairo

2

to Cape Town just because... just because when I was nine I watched a movie about a boy who lived with his parents in Aden. He was out playing in the garden when a bomb fell on his home. The next thing he knew, his parents were being taken away in an ambulance. He was all alone, except for an aunt who lived in Durban. He decided to walk there, 3102 miles away. He slept under trees, stole food, was adopted by strangers, each with their own motive, sometimes good and sometimes bad. He danced with death a thousand times, saw snakes slither by, and lions and elephants stalking the savanna. Yes, he did make it to Durban, but that part I did not care about. As a little girl from Dar-es-salaam, I decided that when a bomb hit our house and my parents got carried away in an ambulance, I would walk to London, for I did have an aunt who lived there. I would camp out with the Bedouins and learn about the secret lives of women who hide behind black veils. I would climb the pyramids and the Tower of London. I wanted to be an adventurer when I grew up, and told my daddy so. He just laughed, but over time he gently steered me into settling for a more conventional life.

That yearning to do something adventurous still lurked in the depths of my being, popping like popcorn, time and time again. I was so ready to do something brave or challenging or stupid.

"Let us join the Peace Corps," I said to my husband, David. "They offer all those opportunities, don't they?" I did not even care where they sent us, though someplace warm would be nice. Fortunately, David was on the same page as I was.

First I had to become an American citizen, a minor detail. I aced the civics test and within a few months I was asked to raise my right hand and swear to defend and uphold the Constitution, so help me God. I did not know it at the time, but this was the first of four swearing-in ceremonies that I would participate in, taking the same oath that Jefferson, Lincoln and Kennedy had taken. I dedicated my 27 months of service to the memory of my mother.

Why, oh why? That is the question.

"Why do you want to join the Peace Corps?" My husband and I were back to being twenty-two again, writing umpteen grad school application-like essays. What are our aspirations, our qualifications? How do we deal with cross-cultural challenges? What if your partner assimilates faster or is more successful than you, how will you cope? The last was for married applicants only. We were on a roll.

Why indeed did I think I would qualify for Peace Corps? Should I tell them about the eighteen months my husband and I spent in India, where I had only a one burner kerosene stove and had to buy kerosene on the black market? Or should I recount the six months I lived with the Zulus, making handmade paper and papier-mâché masks and bowls, while they told stories of how the white soldiers cut the fingers, one by one, of their babies until they disclosed the whereabouts of their husbands or brothers? Maybe they would be impressed by the volunteer work I have done with Hospice and Kulani Prison in Hawaii and with Pakistani immigrants in the Bay Area over the many years of my life. I chose instead to write about my work with the fighter women in Eritrea, where David and I lived for six months. He was there on a special assignment and I had tagged along.

These fighter women grew up in the trenches during the thirty year war that Eritrea fought with Ethiopia. They bore arms, dug trenches, taught and raised kids, hauled equipment, and did everything else that the men did. They fought for the liberation of their country, which finally happened in 1991. Their reward? No jobs, nobody wanted to marry them, and they were isolated from their home communities. They banded together for survival. At their request, I started with English lessons and then paper-making – two things I knew how to do. They then asked me if I could train them to be teachers and do some fund-raising for them. I protested that I had no background or training qualifying me to do that. They insisted that I had more skills and connections than they, and that was good enough! Taking "no" for an answer was not how these women had helped win the war. Feeling stretched, scared about failing them and myself, I embarked on an intense, convoluted journey of teaching myself and gathering resources. The women never let me give up, and together we achieved some of their goals of acquiring skills and becoming self-sufficient. Those six months turned out to be one of the crown jewels of my life's experiences. That was just the kind of adventure I was seeking, living and working in places with few or no resources, and where people are filled with heart and laughter. I would just have to persuade Peace Corps that I believe I have what it takes to be a volunteer, in less than five hundred words.

Our applications were in. We soon received that ominous generic note saying *Thank you for applying... PS.. don't call us, we'll call you.* Lucky us, we did not have to wait long before "The Interview."

Waiting

It was strange being interviewed by someone young enough to be my youngest child. Indeed, for the first time the president of the country was younger than I. How did all these kids manage to land grown-up jobs?

5

It was a breeze to wow the interviewer kid, who had served in Eastern Europe and learned there how to drink schnapps early in the morning. She asked the same questions that were in the application – reasons for wanting to serve as a Peace Corps Volunteer; how have I dealt with cross-cultural issues; and what were my future goals. There were no surprises there, but my patience was about to be tested and I didn't yet know it.

Waiting to hear back from Peace Corps was like waiting for an indefinitely delayed flight, where a prerecorded message plays over and over, apologizing for the delay and appreciating our co-operation and patience. One month, two months went by; still no word, but they appreciated our patience and understood our frustration, so they told us each time we called Washington. Month three came and went and there was still no word.

In the middle of month four, the phone rang at five in the morning. The choice words that were quite ready to spill out of my mouth, letting the caller know in no uncertain terms that this was still the middle of the night in Hawaii, were instantly silenced as my brain registered the words "Peace Corps." She had my attention and my heart pumping.

"Congratulations! You have been nominated to serve in Eastern Europe!"

She needed to know right NOW if we would accept. *Chatteringly, shiveringly icy winters without heat* was my first thought. The only preference we had shown on our applications was for WARM COUNTRIES. How Eastern Europe fit into that category escapes me. I suppose they have a few warm months there, but still... We took a deep breath, looked at each other questioning-ly... and said YES. After the adrenalin rush subsided, the reality of *What have we done!* began to sink in. Maybe they will send us somewhere else. She did say that there was a 50% chance of that happening. But we were in, and that was what counted.

On to the next step – the dreaded blood tests, poop tests, pap smears, chest X-rays, mammograms and dental reports. We were pricked and prodded, poked and measured. Somehow I had managed to get to age 57 without ever having had a complete physical or medical checkup. My only visit to the doctor had been to have some warts burned off. My imagination ran wild with the possibilities of what the tests might churn up. Genetically, I come loaded with predispositions to cancers and heart conditions. Too many of my friends went in for routine checkups and came home with unpronounceable diseases they didn't know they had. I really didn't want and still don't want to know if I have cancer or anything else major. I chewed my fingernails to the cuticles, waiting for the results. "Dear God let there not be anything wrong," I pleaded, wishing I believed in a God who took care of me in that way.

Believer or not, somebody listened. The worst thing the manic medics and dentics could find was one bad tooth in David's mouth that had to be pulled. Not bad for a man who hadn't been to the dentist in 10 years. Other than that we were declared hale and hearty. Hallelujah!

Immediately we put our house on the market. I was in my mean mood. Slash and burn became my mantra as we threw out, gave away and sold those just-in-case extra chairs, the boxes of ceramic tile bought for projects that never materialized, and enough scrap wood and nails to build a castle. The days simply evaporated. We were on the real estate roller coaster, bouncing from hope to despair and back with each showing and offer that came in. Too quickly, the house sold! Holy roller, we were homeless and in Peace Corps Limbo, still waiting to be assigned. It could be many months; and there were no guarantees of where and when we would go, even though we had been nominated to serve in Eastern Europe. All that meant was, there was at least one country that could use our skills. It was tough to place couples with different skill sets.

"Don't quit your day jobs or do anything drastic until we place you," they warned.

Too late!

Homeless and on the road.

What else could we do but mooch off our friends and relatives for a while? We had a glorious time, traveling on Amtrak, visiting his aunt, my aunts, our many friends, his dad, our nephews, his sister and my cousin. We wined and dined and laughed and talked and shopped. We were in the Bay Area for Thanksgiving when the phone call came.

"How good is your French?" the recruiter asked.

Our brains dipped into their memory banks – couldn't find a single Eastern European country that spoke French. OMG! We looked at each other and silently mouthed *Must be West Africa!* There was a cohort departing on January 31st, David's 60th birthday.

"YES! YES!" we said as loudly as we could, before she could change her mind. I had no idea how much I had longed and hoped that we would wind up on the African continent, the landmass on which I took my first breath and swam in the mangrove swamps. I would live in a mud hut with a thatched roof and no electricity or running water. I was bursting with fantasies of my new African adventure, and was already mentally scanning my wardrobe for clothes and shoes to take. We had better practice our French. I wonder if they sell Sensodyne in West Africa? Lists, and lists of lists began to form. We were bound for Mali, home to Timbuktu. How much more exotic can you get!

Four days later, Al Qaeda and Mali were headline news; ten people kidnapped and one Frenchman killed. Normally this news item would fly right by me, except we were due to leave in January to live there for the next 27 months. Oh my goodness, might they actually cancel the program? We called Washington.

"Your safety comes first," Peace Corps assured us. So far the incidents had been in the far northern part of the country, in the desert. It would not affect the program. "Nothing to worry about," they said, and we believed them. We wanted to believe them.

With eight weeks to go, we returned to Hawaii to get packing for our African Adventure. Al Qaeda or not, here we come!

Potty Training 101

Each day here has been a lifetime of experiences. Our life in Hawaii feels like a movie we saw long ago. It is so hard to believe that we first arrived here just 3 weeks ago, I wrote home.

Getting through the airport was a breeze. Packed into a fleet of white land cruisers and vans, we skirted around the capital city of Bamako, barely able to see out, for it was night already. Still we wanted to sponge it all up, the lone pedestrian in a long white robe or the outlines of crumbling buildings lit by dangling, naked, fifteen watt bulbs, giving the impression that the buildings were suffering from severe depression. The town had already shut down. Remnant smoke from cooking fires drifted upward, toward the dark hazy sky.

The PC volunteer in the van handed out water bottles and mosquito repellant sticks with a gentle "put this on NOW, since you have not started on your malaria prophylaxis." Instant, fearful thoughts of angry diseases and virulent rivers blunted the thrill of being here, but just for a moment. Our attention was focused entirely on the escort volunteer who twisted herself behind the seat belt in front to face our expectant and anxious faces. We so desperately wanted to be instantly acclimated and immersed into our new lives, we bombarded her with questions – Do we really get to live in a mud hut? Are the people easy to work with? How welcome are the volunteers? I clung and hung onto every word she said, sucking in her wisdom and experience like a hungry baby at her mother's breast. Forty minutes later we were dropped off at Tubaniso, the Peace Corps training campus outside town.

Our digs at Tubaniso

In the dark, the warm African air felt so good as we strolled down the dimly-lit pathways, clusters of little round huts with thatched roofs on either side. We had the momentary delusion that we had arrived at some exotic resort to begin our African Adventure. Yes indeed, we might just run into Katherine Hepburn and Humphrey Bogart. I was on a private high of *We Are Really Here*. Our Peace Corps lives have begun. We were shown to our rooms and then asked to gather for our first lesson in African survival skills. How to kill snakes and scorpions? Noooooo. It was potty training – how to use those itty bitty rooms, open to the sky and with a little hole in the ground.

I had a sick feeling in my stomach as I gingerly crouched down over that hole in the dark, shooing flies, holding my breath, trying to ensure minimum contact with the floor or walls or anything in that odorous cell, as if the whole building were some kind of gruesome and infectious leper. Holy momma, my aim misfired! That hole was not big enough to pee and poop into at the same time. Enough said. I don't need to tell you about the fragrant consequences of 64 trainees learning by trial and error to use it, this most primitive of arrangements. Yes indeed, Potty Training 101 it was.

No, this was not some resort with warm towels and little soaps and shampoos in bamboo baskets, a bottle of champagne on ice, and a white uniformed African calling us Bwana and Memsahib, catering to our whims with a beautiful smile. This was boot camp.

A spartan bed with a thin sheet, a blanket, a bucket, a pitcher, a whisk broom and four hooks on the wall was what we got. By then the toll of the long journey from Washington DC, the reality of what we were in for, and that lovely warm air began to stifle us. Exhausted we fell into bed... Ouch! The slats cut right through the mattress into my pelvis. Thank God for Melatonin! It was 1:00 am Malian time; breakfast was at eight.

Basic Training

Since that night, much has happened. For one, I now squat down as though it were the most natural thing in the world to do. Not only do I love my newly-developed powerhouse thighs, I also love being a part of this group of trainees, most of whom are in their twenties. They are very smart and energetic, and so ready to give their best to the world.

Long gone is the *OMG what have we signed up for, and for how long?* sinking feeling I had on that first night. How quickly I thought it completely normal to take a bucket bath, to hand wash my clothes after a long day of intensive training, and to sweep up the roaches and sand and whatever else flew in and died on the cement floor of our mud hut. How quickly we fell into the rhythm of the Peace Corps Boot Camp. No, they didn't painfully harden our soft bodies; but our soft minds, used to easy living, convenience, cold beer, hot showers and instant access, were taxed to the max. I don't think my brain has ever had to work this hard and take in so much new information for so long – it hurts!

We're way beyond *This is how you go potty*. We have had lessons on the Do's and Dont's of eating, like:

1. Men and women eat out of separate bowls.

2. Wait for the oldest person to start eating first. However, as a guest you may be asked to go ahead first. If so, please proceed.

3. Eat out of the bowl from the portion directly in front of you. Eat only with your right hand.

4. If there is meat/potatoes/vegetables in the center of the bowl, take only your share by picking off a little bit. Do not eat the whole thing.

5. Do not wait for older people to finish eating before leaving the bowl. Stop eating when you are full. It is not necessary to talk during a meal.

We've had lessons on what to say, do and think in all kinds of unimaginable situations. What do you do if you are stalked? What if you work your butt off to host a workshop and nobody shows up? What if your bike breaks down in the middle of noplace? Or your body? The one that really got our attention was the *What do you do if you find yourself defecating a 10-inch tape worm!* Dr. Dawn put the fear of dying a long and slow and very gruesome death into us, to compel us all to be extraordinarily conservative about hygiene, and stay healthy.

And so it came to pass that, only five days after setting foot in Mali, and armed only with our new cell phones, water filtration systems, a mosquito net, an armful of vaccinations and the Bambara vocabulary for "Good morning, how's your family, goodbye and God Bless," we were ferried to our respective homestay villages for the language and cultural immersion part of training.

I would be lying if I said I wasn't apprehensive. Whenever I am afraid I think of my mother, who was both fearful and courageous at the same time. She would have been horrified at the thought of her daughter living in an African hut, having to carry her own water on her head, no less.

"Your father sacrificed so much to give you a good education, and now you want to live like the Africans?"

I can see her pursing her lips, scrunching her face, disapproval leaking out of every pore, wanting desperately to knock some sense into her mule of a daughter. She would be pleading and praying to her Good Lord, as she called Allah, every moment, every day to abort this adventure; but failing that... "Dear God, please keep her safe, because, well, you know how Africans are!" At the same time she would have been proud that I had the courage to go work amongst the poorest of the poor.

Growing up in Dar-es-Salaam in the fifties, with relative wealth, we had African servants to clean, garden, kill and cook the live chicken that was to be our dinner. To be honest, I never once made a bed or washed a dish until I went to boarding school in

Nairobi. Our servants were housed in mangy cells in the back of the house – sort of an instant ghetto. We knew these people came from villages, but we had never set foot in one. We feared and enslaved them with the blessing of our British colonizers. We could only imagine the squalor and poverty of their living conditions. Our imaginations painted the ugliest pictures of Africans in the colonial Tanganika Territory, as it was known then. They were considered sub-human, and were treated as such by both the Brits and the Asians.

Now in Mali, I am going to be living and working with the equivalent of our servants back in their villages, some of them barely subsisting, too poor to afford anything, too ignorant to know about the germ theory of disease, their women dropping swarms of babies... *How do they all fit inside those little huts?* I asked myself. I would soon find out. Was I apprehensive? Moths swarmed in my stomach as I thought of those unwashed hands that would prepare the meals we would eat together with our fingers, out of a common pot. Malians wash their behinds with their left hands; toilet paper is not a part of their bathroom ritual. They only eat with their right hands, but still. I have seen those left hands come up to help the right from time to time. What kinds of near-death experiences would those germs torment me with? Can I truly handle living with very poor and ignorant African villagers?

We had just five days in Tubaniso, the training center, to prepare us for our Peace Corps lives in the homestay villages. We tortured the poor gardeners, the cooks, the drivers, by practicing on them our newly acquired 10-word Bambara vocabulary. Imagine 60 trainees, each greeting you, every day, thrice a day.

I ni sɔgɔma. I ka kɛnɛ wa? Somɔgɔw ka kɛnɛ? Allah ka hɛrɛ ciaya.

Good morning. How are you? How is your family? God bless you.

It is a wonder that any of them ever got any work done. Yet the staff would greet each of the 60 of us with joy and smiles as beautiful as a new moon. They were the best instant family, and the training center the best home. How quickly we settled into our new routines; how quickly deep friendships blossomed as our souls were stripped bare, talking to each other until the early hours of the morning, trying to cope with the realities of what our new lives might hold for us. Already one trainee could not handle it, and asked to be sent back to America.

Preparing to head out to our Homestays.

Now we were about to be evicted from this womb, and sent to our homestay villages for the language and cultural immersion part of our training, where we were to spend the next two months living with Malian families whom we had never met. A fleet of Peace Corps Land Cruisers stood ready to drive us away, our gear loaded on the roof racks. The scene held all the emotion of parents packing the family wagon to drop off their kid at college for the first time.

Homestay

We drove past dusty dilapidated settlements. The outskirts of Bamako was about as picturesque as a neglected, barren mobile home park, with broken-down cars rusting in the yards and makeshift lean-to's with tin roofing threatening to fall at every quake. I barely registered the passing scenery, as desperately I tried to memorize the speech our language and cultural facilitator had written out for me to give in Bambara: *Dugu tigi ka wòro file bonya … I give you this gift because I respect you.*

I was selected to present the gift of Kola nuts to the village headman on our arrival.

These nuts are the same caffeine-laden, bitter nuts that are used in making Coca Cola. They are about the size of a horse chestnut, with mauve flesh inside. Bitter to chew, the nuts are a mild stimulant and leave a buzz on the tongue, so they tell me. I have never tried them. They are also used to keep hunger at bay. The ritual of giving of kola nuts is a sign of respect. In some villages, a young man will take three kolas to his prospective father-in-law when asking for a girl's hand in marriage. Ten kolas might be expected to 'seal the deal,' and a basket of nuts is presented on the marriage.

After two hours we turned onto a tree-lined dirt road, our hopes rising with the canopy of mango trees, fruit-laden but still green. Mud brick walls enclosed courtyards, not so high that we couldn't peek into the life that bustled in the compounds. My fingers twitched and my camera ached to capture the first sights of women in ankle-length fitted skirts with matching tops and headdresses, made from cloth printed with flowers so huge and bright that they popped out at us. With babies attached to their backs they were pounding millet in giant mortars, while young boys played with marbles and little girls drew bucketloads of water from the well. I was not a camera-clicking tourist. I was a volunteer who wanted to assimilate and be accepted. This was impulse control.

Our little group of six had just driven into a National Geographic Special on Africa, where children spill out of nowhere, their black faces and smiles bright enough to light a Christmas tree; hard working noble natives went about their chores, their life stories waiting to be told through rituals, dance, music and storytelling over hundreds of cups of tea. This is a culture untouched by the internet or television; here the red earth compounds were bare, except for the odd chair or stool or bucket and of course the big Neem tree in the middle, under whose shade families took naps, sipped tea and cooked and ate their meals.

All eyes turned to watch our large foreign vehicle bounce along, spinning clouds of red dust. We were the circus that just rolled into town, and the entire village's assortment of ragged, snotty-nosed kids abandoned their marbles, ran after the car, doubling and tripling in numbers, faster than a telegraph could transmit a message, only to stand transfixed in a circle, watching the six of us and our baggage spill out of the now parked van. One by one the women began to appear with young ones on their hips, silently observing. Chairs appeared for us to sit on. More and more villagers gathered. The men clustered on benches under the tree.

I silently studied their staring faces, wondering which one of those men and women I will be living with. I liked the one who was laughing a lot and waving her arms like an Italian. I hope I don't get the dour looking one. I clutched my water bottle for comfort, feeling like a child at the orphanage, waiting, hoping someone wonderful would adopt me.

The drummers drummed.

Decked out in his gold finery, the *dugutigi* (headman) said, "You may have left your homes, but you have come home."

Women chanted and danced, dipping in and out and up and down, in a circle. The music stopped. I presented the kola nuts, causing a squeal of delightful murmur amongst the women who could hear me. "This Toubab speaks Bambara!"

Ha! Little do they know.

Toubab is the generic, sometimes derogatory name originally given to the French colonists but now used for all foreigners. When Malians wanted to get our attention, they would call out "Toubab."

One by one our names were called, and the drum roll began as each of us stepped forward to dance with their new house mother. I was waiting my turn.

An audience with the Dugutigi

"David Drury and the Coulibally family," our Language and Cultural facilitator called. The laughter-filled woman who waved her arms like an Italian stepped forward, as did David. *Lucky him!* I was envious. For the next nine weeks we would be separated, as we were assigned to different families for this portion of the training. Nervously I was scanning the remaining faces, giving each a label – *dour; animated; old; well dressed.*

"Asifa Kanji and Diarra family." My heart jumped. I saw a young woman in rags hand off her baby, looking like she had been pulled from a hard day in the fields. Reluctantly she took the floor, as did I. I danced with all my might to keep my heart from crashing, my brain from thinking. What was I in for?

With my bag on her head, her baby on her back, she silently led the way to the Diarra family compound. I had walked into a Christmas crèche; three goats rested lazily in the shade of a mango tree, while the donkey grazed on the straw. Chickens and chicks clucked, and the raggedy young woman with whom I danced settled herself under the tree with her baby at the breast.

The well, with its bucket tied at the end of the rope, added that extra *je ne sais quoi* to the place. All this totally fulfilled my romantic notion of what my life in Mali would be; I could not have designed the set any better.

What the courtyard lacked was the mandatory swarm of kids bursting to play ball with me, do hi fives, and mercilessly use me like a new toy or a favorite aunt that they could clamber all over. My Malian parents were a very old and infirm retired military man and his fifty year old wife. Their kids had all moved to the big city. They had hired a young couple to live in and look after the old folks, and now me. An eleven year old grand-daughter also lived with them. It was the help that had come to fetch me. This was her first encounter with a foreigner. Thus began my life in this itty bitty village with no electricity, no indoor plumbing and no running water.

Home sweet home

Two minutes was all it took for me to run out of my good-afternoon-how-are-you-god-bless-you vocabulary with my new host family. Goodness only knows what they said next. I just forced a happy, cackly laugh that was meant to say, *whatever it was you said, I am amenable and at your mercy, so please be kind to me as I have no idea about what to do next,* and nodded vigorously as though it was the right thing to do. They stared back, looking quite confused and proceeded to discuss me amongst themselves. It was going to be a long nine weeks. The young woman pointed to my room. I couldn't run away from my awkwardness fast enough. Should I burst into tears or laugh hysterically? How do I cope with this emotional Gordian knot that was growing within me? Slowly my spartan room came into focus. Ah yes, I should unpack and put up the mosquito net and set up the water filter. For the moment, all that helped to reaffirm my capabilities as an adult.

There was a knock at my door. *Oh please God, make this easy for me.* The eleven year old grand-daughter pointed to a pot and a stool under the mango tree. *Yeah so there is a pot and a stool under the mango tree, so what?* She grabbed my hand and led me to it, and un-covered the pot. Steam wafted up from the rice and sauce. I was hungry, but was this supposed to feed all of us? Pantomime and laughter pursued. I gathered that the food was just for me, and they had already eaten. I had an audience who watched me wash my hands and roll a ball of rice with my right hand and put it into my mouth. I gather I passed some kind of test, as everyone but the eleven year old dispersed.

Without any ceremony, my new mother christened me Fatumata, after her eldest daughter. Thus, in village I became Fatumata Diarra, and David, Dauda Coulibaly. Now when we introduced ourselves, everyone knew exactly where and with what family we lived in this truly quaint village, surrounded by rocky crags, mango orchards and vegetable gardens that stretch from the village to the river. This area is the region's fruit and veggie basket, and the majority of the villagers are subsistence farmers.

I Had a Bath This Morning

I love bath time – the feel of cool water drizzling down my sweaty back is absolutely delicious. I don't even dry myself; I let the breeze cool me down. It feels soooo good. My village life is so simple, it is beautiful. I have no chatchkas to dust, food to cook, shopping or laundry to do, or anything. The girl draws the bucketful of water that I use to bathe morning and evening in this bathroom, open to the sky and light of the rising and setting sun.

"Don't look at anyone until you have washed your face in the morning," they drummed in at orientation. "It is downright rude!"

At first it was hard to hide my face on the way to the bathroom and not say good morning to my host mom, who was already pounding the onions and garlic to a mash for our lunch. Face washed, I was bathed again in the sweet downpour of *How are you, did you have a peaceful night, god bless you, god bless your husband, may you have a peaceful day, may god keep you healthy and safe; may you come home safely from class; greet them (the other students) for us,* from every member of my family. I had to allow a good twenty minutes for my morning greetings. My own mother too was a virtuoso blesser. As a kid, I was barely tolerant of her asking God to take care of me and make me successful. I would have much preferred a new dress than a shower of maternal blessings. But at this advanced age, I felt her warmth hugging me so tightly through my Malian family's words.

Our Bambara classroom was nothing more than the shade of a tree for the six of us, in the compound where our language and cultural facilitators lived. As the shade moved, so did we, with our chairs, the blackboard, the box of chalk, notebooks and water bottles.

The Classroom

Namasa ka kilo kelen ye joli ye? How much for a kilo of bananas?

Kɛmɛ. Five hundred francs.

Ayi!! O ka ca! A barika. No! That's too much! Come down a little.

We were learning to bargain in Bambara, doing role play after role play, buying imaginary bananas, sugar and cloth. I would come home for my rice and mystery sauce lunch and ask my host mom,

Jege ye joli ye? How much for the fish?

She was taken aback but humored me anyway. Toubabs ask strange questions.

Keme fila. A thousand francs

O ka ca! I would retort, and she would burst out laughing, clapping her hands, and then repeat what I just said to the girl. Now they both would shake with laughter. I would also tell my family *I had a bath and ate lunch and went to class today*, all in Bambara, just to hear their laughter. Maybe if I flunk out of Peace Corps, I could get a job as a standup comic in Mali.

New words and phrases are flying at me at warp speeds, yet I am still unable to converse with a six year old. How I am going to be able to go to work with my *Hello, I had a bath this morning and then ate breakfast* vocabulary? I'm a little scared; am I too old to learn? Every volunteer goes through this, I console myself. But, but...... says the little voice inside of me, but I am too brain-dead to hear it. I am exhausted, cannot think, cannot learn...... I just want to eat dark chocolate and sip enough red wine to send me into peaceful oblivion. This is just half way through our training. We still have four more weeks to go, and the days are getting hotter and our bodies sweatier.

The Peace Corps folks in Bamako know this drowning point so well that they treated all the trainees to a most mind-renewing few hours, in a place where we could just be Americans. They took us to the American Club in Bamako, where we spent our entire monthly stipend on ice cold beer, hamburgers and a swim.

To speak English, to be understood, to have people laugh at my jokes and not feel dumb, how sweet that was! I discovered I was not alone in my *it is time to give up and go home* thoughts. With my attitude adjusted, I was re-energized for the next phase, which was finding out exactly where we will be serving for the next two years and actually getting to visit it, to meet some of the people we will work with as well as the families we will be staying with. If it is anything like homestay, I will be overjoyed.

Site Visit

"Where would you like to work?" they had asked in a question-naire way back when.

"In a rural village far, far away, where I would carry water on my head and sit around the big mango tree, sipping sweet tea, talking story with my African family." I wrote.

David, on the other hand, mentioned that his professional skills and French would be put to better use in a town, and at 60 he was doubtful about cycling down 10-15 miles of dirt roads in 115 degree heat every day to make business calls. It was the classic clash of my dreams and his reality. Peace Corps and the Universe took his side.

Our new home? The small city of Kayes (pronounced Kai) in western Mali, on the shores of the Sahara, reputed to be the hottest continuously inhabited place in Africa. But lucky us, being in a city we may actually have electricity and running water, which the village volunteers won't. With temperatures already reaching the high nineties, and this at just the beginning of the hot season, the thought of sleeping under a fan was not altogether unwelcome. At 4:00 am, we boarded the bus that took us from Bamako to Kayes, a bumpy ten hour ride, just for a three day site visit.

David had been assigned to a public service radio station, a Malian NPR, as a Small Enterprise Development volunteer. I was to help out at a local clinic as a health volunteer. For the first time we got to visit our respective workplaces, which had put in requests for volunteers many months ago. David was thrilled with his new work situation. Radio Rurale had started some income-generating enterprises to support itself, but needed much more to be self sufficient. I, on the other hand, quaked and cringed about working in a clinic for malnourished babies even before I got to visit it. Would I be able to deal with the heartbreak of handling the fragile skeletons that they call babies? Even if we help save the babies, what will be their quality of life? The moral dilemma haunted me. For the first time since we landed, I literally had a very sick stomach while in Kayes. It refused to process anything I ate, spewing it back out from any and all orifices. That, coupled with not being able to communicate with my Malian counterpart, and the sinking heart disappointment I felt at seeing the accommodations picked out for us, made me want to give up and go home.

"I have found you a palace," our exuberant local coordinator beamed. He was so proud to have found us a cavernous ground floor five room apartment with badly poured concrete floors, tiny windows, and not a closet or a countertop or anything inside – just big bare, dark rooms with one tap outside in the courtyard as the only water source for the building. Across the street from our flat was a shop renting concert-size speakers, blasting the same CD at a million decibels over and over and over. To go to the outhouse, I would have had to pass the rooms of several single men who mostly hang out outside. Can you imagine the scampering I would have had to do should I have a case of the runs? The prospect was fresh in my mind as I endured for the first time what Dr. Dawn called 'Mr. D' (for diarrhea), and what I called the Mali weight loss program. To Malians, this was a palace; to my sinking heart, I was being sentenced to life in down-market urban hell. The coordinator registered our disappointment. Ultimately we'll have to make do with whatever we are issued, but for right now he said he would try to find us something else. As always, time would allow me to lower the expectations I didn't know I had, and then move on to make the most of the situation, but I was not quite there yet. I was still dreaming of village life.

Back to the village we went for the home stretch. We still had four more weeks of language and cultural training.

Our Values Versus Theirs

"Corrupt, poor, uneducated and possibly uneducatable; they have too many children; women have no freedom and are treated very badly; they are good dancers and musicians; eager to help; very family oriented; generous and religious."

This was the list we made of our stereotypes of Malians, in one of our cross-cultural workshops.

Our Malian language and cultural facilitators (LCFs) did the same for Americans. Here's what they thought of us:

"Rich, warriors, independent, patriotic, curious, DIRTY, alco-holic, well organized, hypocrites, scared, homosexuals, badly dressed, gender defenders, non-believers, courageous, and creative." (It was they who capitalized 'dirty,' not me).

Here's what they said about their own Malian values, in order of importance. Their number one value was family and marriage, very closely followed by hospitality and solidarity. Respect for elders and hierarchy were also very important; then came Joking Cousins (more on that later), peace-making and tolerance, followed by ethics and valuing diversity. They shared a popular Malian proverb with us which translates as: "It is better to die than be ashamed."

In contrast, our group of Peace Corps volunteers put down Freedom as their Number One value. Equality and Patriotism came in at second and third, followed by Success and Capitalism. Family came last on this short list.

Was there a potential clash of values and culture here? We thought so. The rest of the workshop was spent coming up with ideas for coping with the differences so that working together would be a successful joint venture. There were strategies like asking why, instead of judging or assuming; we asked our counterparts not to be afraid to tell us when we did something culturally wrong. They asked us volunteers not to be afraid to ask for help, and to be patient with them, because change comes slowly.

Done! Done! Done!

"It is all over!" I wrote in my journal. "We are sooo done with our pre-service training. I am totally ready for a vacation – a swim in the Mediterranean, lazing on the sand, sipping colorful cocktails with umbrellas floating lazily in them."

That was just what I should have ordered, but instead I signed a piece of paper committing myself to two years of service. Silly Asifa! She said she wanted an adventure, something completely different. The Universe responded without reading any of the fine print of her wishes, especially the bit about beach holidays. A tenement apartment in Kayes and starving babies at the clinic was not quite what I had in my mind, but that is the challenge I have been handed. Can I make my life work under these circumstances? Will my work be meaningful and rewarding? How about the badly needed attitude adjustment, will that happen? We shall wait and see.

The last weeks in village were so precious. I truly loved the rhythm of life in my mud hut without electricity and running water. There was so much beauty in the simplicity of the daily routine – from drawing bath water from the well, to squatting down in the courtyard, to hand washing my clothes using a bucket and a wash board that I first mistook for a musical instrument. A lot of squatting, no question about it, but I don't even think about it anymore. Haven't yet learned to balance that basket full of veggies or bucket full of water on my head, though. Two steps was as far as I got before it all came tumbling down, causing my Malian family to crack up with laughter and clap their hands in delight. They were so easy to please. How I hate to be wrenched from this poetic life.

Language-wise, we have gone beyond the *Did you sleep well / I had a bath this morning routine*. Now I can tell you that I am smarter than you in Bambara – though I don't think that will help me to tell mothers to feed their malnourished babies with something other than powdered rice and sugar, or that it is high time they started to give their eighteen month old baby some solid food. Next Monday I start work at the women's health center. So help me God, and please pour into my head all the Bambara words I will need to discuss with the mothers the welfare of their children, like *Boil the water before you give it to your baby. Diarrhea comes from germs.* – But then how does one begin to describe what a germ is?

The Test

It was time for the scary final language test, before being allowed to swear in as full Volunteers. We would have to hold a conversation in Bambara with a native speaker for half an hour, which had me agonizing over what failure looks like. Took me right back to primary school, where my teacher had a pointy hat fashioned from old crinkled brown wrapping paper that had a large letter D for DUNCE written on it. With it, she would crown the head of anyone who had not done their homework and made them stand in the corner of the classroom, facing the rest of the students. It never happened to me, but it could now.

My fifty-eight year old brain struggled so hard to retain vocabulary and phrases that might as well have been utter gibberish. Every night, while the young volunteers partied and played, I sweated under my mosquito net, repeating the vocabulary over and over, until the batteries in my flashlight burned out. On those hot nights sleep was hard to come by, so I deprived myself further by holding mental conversations in Bambara with the phantom souls of my mind.

I am NOT too old for this, I can do it, I can do it, I kept trying to convince myself.

And I did. David and I had the dubious distinction of being the first "old people" to pass the test first time around in many years. Even if I forget all my Bambara, I hope that the agony of learning killed off plenty of my Alzheimer cells, a reward that would be worthwhile in itself.

From Trainee to Volunteer

From the Presidential Palace you cannot smell the open sewers, or breathe in the dust, or see the billions of used plastic bags that litter Bamako. From that perch on a high hill overlooking the city, Bamako is a toy town of miniature houses and buildings draped alongside the majestic Niger river. From up there Bamako is positively leafy, a most inviting place for those who enjoy a peaceful, friendly stroll. You cannot hear the roar of motorbikes on unpaved roads, smell the exhaust, or imagine the squalor or bustle of people, kids and wares. You cannot see how life and death lie side by side in the heart and soul of the city.

Across the green manicured palace lawns, sixty-one of us strutted and strolled like grads to our senior prom, decked out in all our finery. In the last days of training, both men and women searched the markets for bazan, a locally dyed and waxed fabric in countless hues of yellows and reds and blues, used for special occasions. We crowded tailors' shops, fabric in hand, trying to explain in Bambara just how we wanted our long fitted skirts with matching tops and headdresses sewn and embroidered. It was not just the women; the men too got into designing their boubous, the long flowing kaftans. We were the belles and beaux at our swearing-in ceremony at the Presidential Palace.

Joining us were four hundred invited guests, ranging from embassy staff and USAID folks, to Malian cabinet ministers and various and sundry muckety mucks, our village hosts, and of course Monsieur Le Président himself.

For the Malians the high point was the speeches given by our five valedictorians, who wrote and delivered their five minute addresses in the local languages that they were studying (Bambara, Kasonke, Malinke, Dogon and Fulani). Each of the speakers packed in humor and blessings and gratitude, and quite obviously knocked the socks off the audience. *These Americans have been here for ten weeks?*

Even the President smiled at the jokes aimed at him. He got up and said without reservation that Peace Corps, its mission and its volunteers were the best gift America offers the developing and underdeveloped world, and thanked us for going out into the remote villages and lending our lives and expertise to enable the Malian people.

The President was a warm, friendly, unassuming man: if you passed him by on the street you'd peg him for a kindly old high school teacher. Nothing about his simple white robe or his bearing gave away his Presidential status, or reminded us that he was once the soldier who toppled a dictatorial regime in 1992, set up a democratic caretaker government, and then stepped aside. It was a pleasure and an honor shaking his hand and having a group picture taken with him.

A tear-provoking lump swelled in my throat as the United States Ambassador to Mali spoke:

> *They are the best that America has to offer the world. I salute their courage, their enthusiasm, and generosity. I cannot imagine a better way to show the American people's collective commitment to working hand-in-hand with the people of Mali...*

And when our country director said,

> *These Americans come with the desire to work toward the noble causes of peace and development, as well as for the ideal of mutual understanding across cultures...*

Tears were rolling down my cheeks. I was part of something so much bigger. I was part of that dream that JFK had when he started the Peace Corps back in 1961. I was no longer this 58 year old woman from Hilo, Hawaii who just wanted an adventure. The words *courage, generosity, noble causes of peace,* made me so much bigger, like I might have been Florence Nightingale herself, or Nelson Mandela. I let those tears flow as my little middle-aged adventure became a calling. Never have I felt so humble, and yet so happy to be a part of it.

Madame Ambassador then asked us to stand and promise before God and these witnesses that we will carry out our duty as Peace Corps Volunteers. She asked us to raise our right hands and repeat after her:

I do solemnly swear that I will support and defend the constitution of the United States against all enemies foreign and domestic, and that I will bear true faith and allegiance to the same, that I take this obligation freely, without any mental reservation or purpose of evasion, and that I will well and faithfully discharge my duties in the Peace Corps, so help me God.

Each of the volunteers was given a white rose, and the presidential staff wheeled in a cake with sparklers to celebrate the 50th anniversary of Peace Corps and 40 years of continuous service in Mali. I loved dressing up; I loved the pomp and circumstance. I let those tears dribble down to my smiling lips as people congratulated us on our courage and selflessness. After this we had better get out there and do something worthwhile! It was an evening that pressed all the inspiration buttons.

The President, and the Kennedys

Christening the New Volunteers

At Tubaniso, we had our last supper together. The kitchen staff set the tables outside under the African sky and served finger lickin' fried chicken and French fries. Thank you Peace Corps staff; thank you language and cultural facilitators; thank you kitchen and ground staff and drivers; thank you volunteers for mentoring us, taking care of us and allowing us to cry on your shoulders for these last nine weeks of training. As the tributes flowed, there was a sense of sadness, like a family breaking up. We were birds in a nest, ready to fly. By this time tomorrow, we would be scattered all across the country in the villages where we would live and work for the next two years.

One of the long-standing traditions of Peace Corps Mali is that the seasoned volunteers who help to train the new group or *stage* (rhymes with garage) get the honor of christening it. The young, fresh-faced group before us, who trained last July, were dubbed "Team America," and the cohort before them were the famous "Risky Business" – so called because they were damned competent at what they did, but had a reputation for testing the limits of any and all Peace Corps rules.

The grads of April 2011? We will be known as "The Kennedys." As the senior PCV trainers tell it, there were three reasons for the name. For starters, we have been given Royal treatment all the way. At our orientation in Washington, the Malian ambassador and the head of Peace Corps regaled us with their presence, and of course our swearing-in was witnessed by the President of Mali. Not only that, our stage somehow wrangled free Peace Corps transport for shopping sprees and visits to the tailor, privileges which were not afforded to previous, less aristocratic stages. The second reason is that, like the Kennedys, the 61 of us acted like a close-knit family, not a collection of cliques. And of course they wanted to honor the golden anniversary of an organization that was inaugurated by the most famous Kennedy of all.

As we begin our lives as volunteers, David and I will be staying at the Stage house in Kayes, as the regional coordinator has been unable to find us suitable digs. Stage houses are PC houses in the regional capitals where village volunteers can come once a month to do their banking, catch up with e-mail, Facebook, Skype home, eat hamburgers and be American for a couple of days. The Kayes house is air conditioned (well, one room is), has round the clock internet service, and an incredible library of books and movies. Living there will not be a sacrifice. If I cannot live in a mud hut, then an air conditioned room will suite me just fine. The temperatures now are in the hundreds.

Tomorrow we have good intentions of reporting to work!

The First Three Weeks

It has been an *I-desperately-want-out-of-here* kind of few weeks. I would have been long gone, had it not been for the sheer pleasure of gorging on soft fleshy mangoes with juice dribbling down my arms to my elbows, then licking the sweet nectar from what is left on my sticky fingers. Every morning I have been making myself go to the dowdy Women's Health Center. Once in its life, the building must have been a smart and gracious colonial residence, with pillars holding up the front porch and a flowered walkway leading up to it. Today the paint is too tired and dirty to stick to the walls. The rooms are furnished with a mishmash of decaying chairs, benches, tables and beds. Boxes of supplies are carelessly strewn about. The old bedrooms are now delivery rooms, consulting rooms, and storerooms. The smallest room in the front of the house had bars across the windows. It became the pharmacy.

I watched a baby being born – a very first for me, and I am definitely not in any rush to return to the delivery room. I do not think that they will invite me back after my Hollywood swoon. I could see the crown of the baby's head emerge. The laboring mother was writhing and pushing. *Come on baby, come out! Come! Come!* I was wishing with all my heart. Then my eyes darted to the Matrone (the midwife) as she nonchalantly grabbed a pair of surgical scissors and without so much as a by your leave, just snipped the vagina of the birthing mother. No anesthetic, no antiseptic or disinfectant to clean the area, no warning, just snip. The last thing I remember was the mother's tortured scream.

I never had any children of my own, and after this experience, I am not about to encourage anybody else to do so! I have often wondered if the reason I chose not to have kids had to do with my mother telling me, over and over, that in another life she would not have had children. I am happy she had me, but I have never had the urge to have a child. Unlike my mother, I had a choice.

In my twenties I rationalized that there are too many kids in the world to bring forth yet another. That opinion gained strength when we lived in India. One day as I sat at my typewriter, tap-tapping away, I heard a child give out a heart-piercing yelp. Of course I went out to check. My neighbor, who also came out, explained that it was a mother chopping the fingers off of her baby.

"Whaaaaat?"

"She was doing her child a favor," he explained.

With his maimed hand, he would command a bigger income as a beggar and thus not go hungry! At that moment I knew I would not have a baby of my own.

It is ironic that I am now in Mali educating mothers about the importance of breast feeding, and adding protein to the diets of their children once they have been weaned. I cannot grasp how it is that women have been getting pregnant and giving birth for well over 100,000 years, and yet they know so little about child rearing. Surely every community has a bosom of wise grannies to guide women through their pregnancies, help them with the birth and advise new mothers on the ABC's of baby care. In present-day Mali, a woman has an average of seven pregnancies, adding half a million people a year to the population. So many babies to practice on, and yet many mothers do not have a clue.

It is not unusual for a woman to purposely fast in her ninth month, just so that the baby would be smaller, making it easier to birth. Only two babies in ten are exclusively breast-fed in the first six months. Can mothers not correlate that their babies are not growing because mum feeds them nothing but a watery, sugary rice porridge with no protein or vegetables whatsoever, often until the babies are almost two?

I was baffled by so many of the village beliefs, like the entrenched idea that malaria comes from eating mangos. I also discovered that many people do not wash their hands with soap and water after going to the bathroom or before preparing food or eating, because there is some superstition that washing your hands with soap washes away your good fortune. Making them believe in the existence of germs, these unseeable things that cause diarrhea, is as challenging as convincing a die-hard atheist of the existence of God.

Children dying is such a frequent occurrence that it's come to be expected. It is, after all, the will of Allah. Well over half the entire population of Mali (14.8 million), is under the age of eighteen, of which 13% won't live to see their fifth birthday.[1]

Almost four out of ten kids suffer from chronic under-nutrition. Needless to say, contraception is not a part of their reality. Less than ten percent of reproductive age women use it.

What horrified me most were the statistics on genital mutilation of daughters: 75% of baby girls are 'circumcised.' Most families, including the women, approve of the practice. It is totally beyond my comprehension why a woman would do that to her daughter. It is something that *women* do, with or without the consent of men. I have heard too many stories about modern dads who will not let their young daughters spend time with grandma, for fear that they will be surreptitiously taken away, and mutilated.

That's the real Peace Corps world – the workplace where I am to make a difference. It's where I have discovered just how incompetent I really am. I understand so little of what anybody is saying to me, so I laugh and nod a whole lot, like a blithering deaf-mute idiot. Mute because my Bambara vocabulary is nothing to write home about, despite passing the PC test. The sentence I really need to learn is *I am only stupid when I speak Bambara, but in English I am really quite smart. Just ask me!* The million-dollar question is, will I *ever* get smart in Bambara? What made me think I could ever learn this language?

Just the same, I show up at the health center every morning at 8:00 am and sit silently on the bench against the wall in the circle of ten to fifteen health staff working that day, listening to the turnover reports from the night nurses to the day shift. Somewhere I have this little bit of faith in myself, that if I keep going and keep making a fool of myself with my baby talk, somehow, some day, I will magically be a fully functioning

[1]http://www.unicef.org/infobycountry/mali_statistics.html

volunteer there. I am apt to take wild guesses at what is being said and respond accordingly. They tolerate me as they would a retarded child, with pity and gentle forbearance. Mostly the staff ignore me, especially after the initial curiosity wore off. I get the distinct feeling that the Chef de la Poste (the Doctor in charge) is very disappointed, because the last volunteer, who was fluent in French and more seasoned as a volunteer, hit the ground running. I, on the other hand, appear to be a stalled car that cannot be jump started. Believe me he tries, with volleys of questions. I can only shrink and reply *dɔɔni dɔɔni* (slowly slowly) – but he is long gone, muttering and shaking his head.

Women waiting to be seen

I tried my hand at weighing a few babies under the tired and totally uninterested supervision of Fanta, the junior nurse in charge, who wouldn't even get up to read the hanging scale at eye level. From her sitting-down perspective the kids come in at half a kilo lighter than what they really are, but she does not care. How do I work in spite of her attitude – or better still, how do I change her attitude? My heart broke over and over as I held one fragile, scrawny baby after another. One of them was so small that he fit in the palms of my hands, his eyes staring at me, almost motionless but desperate. Dear God have mercy on these souls. I went home crying.

The germ theory of disease is as far from these 'professional' health workers' minds as Pluto is from Earth. The woman doing vaccinations breaks open the little plastic serum tube with her teeth, spits the cap on to the floor and then squeezes the contents into each of the babies' mouths. There is no sink or soap nearby. Is there any hope for these infants to survive both the poverty and ignorant incompetence they have been born into? Who am I to save these babies so that they can lead half-starved lives? Just how many people do we have to touch before this country will reach its tipping point?

It does not help that we are stuck in this rubbish heap of a town, where we are not a part of any community. It does not help my despair to think how hard it will be to become assimilated. Unlike the village volunteers, we do not have host families; our counterparts barely have time for us. There is one cell somewhere in my brain that says, "Stick with it despite your disgust at how much Bambara you have already lost. Concentrate on what you remember, and trust that it will all come together." But then the other voice says, "give up, there is no light at the end of the tunnel." In fact there is no tunnel – just a deep dark hole. Well, at least it is an air-conditioned hole!! From hope to despair I swing.

Super Saviors

Even though we are assigned to one organization, there is much else that a volunteer can do.

"Look at the community as a whole, and work with them to assess their needs and promote self-help projects in line with their priorities," they drummed into us at training. But that is not all. There are several other agendas we are supposed to incorporate into our work if we can: Food Security being one, Gender and Development (the new politically correct term for fighting to give women a better deal in a society) being another; not to mention cultural exchange, education, environmental and income-generating projects. We are to "facilitate an integrated approach to development which is self sustaining." It all sounded so good and feasible in training. It spoke to the superhero in me.

Super volunteers abound. There was one who had enabled her village of 1200 to build 136 wastewater soak-pits, started an art program for the kids, coaches a girls' soccer team, and has a gardening project going. That's just what she gets done before breakfast... and she's only been here seven months!

I poured my heart out to one of the volunteers who had been here a while.

"Stop moaning and do something else," she said.

"You mean I can totally skip going to the health center?" My mind ran to the Dunce hat on my teacher's desk.

An emphatic "Yes!" came the answer.

"Would I not be letting the health center down?" I asked, with a little bit of hope creeping into my voice.

Mismatches between the volunteer and the service they are assigned do occur, and of course it is possible to change assignments. Maybe I knew this, but I have never not risen to a challenge and made good my commitment. This was a first. Having said that, from the bottom of my heart, I truly did not want to work at the health center, weighing starving babies. If I left the CSCOM (health center), what would I do? What did I want my Peace Corps service to be? The wheels in my brain began to churn, and I began to look for other opportunities.

My mother, the compulsive do-gooder whom I spent my whole life criticizing, is manifesting in Asifa. This wanting to feel useful, wanting to do for others, wanting to improve the lot for others is as much a part of me as it was of her. What drove her drives me, but she did it the only way she knew how – by being a benefactress, and a servant of God. I remember the guilt I tried to lay on her, when one of her charity cases got pregnant for the fifth time by an abusive, drunken, good for nothing husband who stole what little money she earned from cleaning toilets at a hotel. She asked for help. My mum and her rich friends would not raise the money to send her to a private abortion clinic, get her counseling, or help her get a restraining order against the husband

"She's illegal, she might get deported," came the fearful refrain. Being sent back to Pakistan would be worse than staying in an abusive relationship.

"Never mind," my mother would try to appease me. "I will make sure the baby has enough food, and will go to school."

My mother, bless her soul, bore the financial responsibility for that child all the way through college, as well paying the school fees for the next child.

I don't want to pay for anyone's college education, but how do I build capacity in others so that they may help themselves? The question rolled around and around in my head like beads in a rattle.

Moving Forward

I rummaged through the library at the Stage House, home to many a manual and starter kit left by previous volunteers: *Teaching Your Community About HIV Aids; How to Make Soap and Neem Cream; Fighting Malnutrition with Moringa.* The latter caught my eye. Everything you ever wanted to know about Moringa but were afraid to ask, from what is it to how to grow and eat it, with texts in English, French and Bambara. Moringa, the miracle tree whose leaves cure whatever it is that ails you – malnutrition to arthritis to eczema, the literature said. My brain was doing cartwheels, spinning ideas of how I would start the First Church of Moringa and preach its virtues. I would help them grow the tree right in the CSCOM courtyard. We could process it and give the powder to mothers to add to the rice porridge they feed their babies, and voila! I could single handedly wipe out malnutrition in Kayes on no budget, since the seeds are donated by the PC/USAID food security program.

The next day, I left the house singing, *Hi Ho, Hi Ho, it's off to the CSCOM I go.* Whenever any of the staff looked like they needed company, I pulled out the Bambara paragraph extolling the virtues of Moringa and cornered them into listening.

Moringa nursery at the Stage House

"Moringa has all kinds of micro- and macro-nutrients, and is the only leaf that contains ALL the amino acids. Gram for gram it contains the protein of an egg, four times the vitamin A of carrots, four times the calcium of milk, three times the potassium of bananas; and seven times the vitamin C of oranges. It is like growing a vitamin tree at your door," I extolled. "What is more, it grows well in Kayes…"

Soon I had at least one convert, and a couple more sounded impressed! I was on a roll, and immediately planted about twenty seeds in the PC Stage house garden. I was climbing out of my AC hole. We hired a school teacher to help us with our Bambara three days a week and, the best news of all, our regional coordinator found us an apartment.

Bin Laden

Beep, beep, beep, both our cell phones nagged, very early in the morning. A text message from Peace Corps:

> *Pls don't manifest in public. FYI Bin Laden killed. Thx!*

Our Inbox had messages from the Embassy and from our Country Director, all asking us to keep a low profile and go out as little as possible until they could suss out how the news was being received locally. We did not see signs of any negative reaction. It was just another lethargically sweaty day in the hot season.

I personally have such mixed feelings. Revenge is sweet in light of the pain caused, but in my gut I wonder what the world would be like if we did not kill or take joy in killing our enemies, and forgave them instead. For me, it was a day of reflection and meditation. I thought back to the time in South Africa when I lived among the Zulus, listening to stories about the Apartheid years that made me want to run out and torture every Afrikaaner who crossed my path. The Zulu ladies tried to calm my fury. If Madiba (Nelson Mandela) can forgive his torturers, surely, so can we. Lily Tomlin hit the nail on the head when she said, "Forgiveness means giving up all hope of a better past."

Joking Cousins

Who are your joking cousins? One finds out very quickly. It is part and parcel of the Malian greeting ritual, which goes something like this:

Good Morning

How are you?

Did you have a peaceful night?

How is your family? Your children? Your husband? etc... (This part can go on for a long time.)

What is your name?

What is your family name?

Then, depending on your family name, the greeter will either express great satisfaction at your choice of parentage, or make a face showing total disgust – like how could you possibly belong to that ragtag bean- or donkey-eating crew – and say "They are terrible people!" To which you answer with much alacrity that it is *their* clan that farts too much or whatever other clever insults you can come up with in the moment. This is always met with a rebuttal and so much genuine laughter that you can't help but laugh too.

This extremely well-scripted mirthful charade lasts a minute or two or three, but at the end of it rapport and friendship have been established. The ice is beyond broken; it has melted away.

If their family name is the same as yours, you promptly establish brother or sisterhood by congratulating each other on your fine pedigree – "You're another!" – and the conversation moves on.

The thing that really gets me (and all other foreigners) is that these friendly insults and bean-eating hundred year old fart jokes are exchanged *each time you see someone*, more or less, every day for generations. The Malians never tire of it; what is even more hilarious is that they find the same joke that they have told and heard a gazillion times truly funny. The good news is that every greeting is accompanied by laughter. We go along with the program.

Who gets to joke with whom? Believe it or not, there is a list! Diarras (my clan) only get to joke with the Traores. The Coulibalys (David's family name) get to joke with just about everyone, and are widely accused of being the biggest bean eaters in the world. I mean to say the only reason I, a Diarra (which means lion), buy and cook beans is to satisfy my Coulibaly husband. Personally I never touch the stuff, and try to endure my husband's farts with as much compassion as I can. Am I a long suffering wife or what! We all know my husband is full of gas, don't we? You get the gist, and I'm sure David has his own very skewed and possibly cleverer version of the same story. That's how the Coulibalys are. A fact of Malian life.

[Pay no attention to this woman; a Diarra is exactly the kind of person who would fart in an elevator – well OK Mali doesn't actually have any elevators, but they'd fart in them if they could – and then glare at some decent guy like it was his fault. That's Diarras all over. I'll set you straight in some later letter. –Ed.]

The Joking Cousins tradition stems back to stories from the days of yore. In one such story, a village saved another from something quite dreadful and life-threatening, at some cost to itself. The indebtedness created a deep bond of cousinhood between the clans. However, that bond came at a price, where people who were saved were teased about being lazy good for nothings, and that all they did was to eat beans all day.

Another more popular story is of a King who created an empire, but played it absolutely fair by giving the same privileges to those he conquered as he afforded his own people, so that they would live in peace with each other. The conquered people expressed eternal gratitude to their new cousins for generations to come. However, they had to put up with all kinds of good humored insults, such as your tribe eats donkey – hahahha! The teasing and one-upmanship about each other's less than refined habits kept them amused, and became a fun ritual which continues on until today.

Greetings aside, to this day Malians uphold their dedication to each other as joking cousins, as was illustrated by a personal story told by our own language teacher, a Coulibaly. He was in an auto accident. The other driver was absolutely furious, threatening and on the verge of calling the police (a major no-no here – you only do that to your worst enemy). As luck would have it, our teacher was recognized by a passerby who yelled out his name. "Eh Coulibaly!" At this point the furious driver chilled. His threats turned to insults about what bad drivers those lousy bean eating Coulibalys were, and that they should all have their licenses taken from them. That was the clue that told our teacher that the guy whose car he hit was a joking cousin, bonded to his clan by their distant past and bound to maintain the peace between them. The police were not called; they settled amongst themselves and they went out and had tea together.

And so it is that Malians spend the whole day greeting and telling fart and bean jokes to each other. This is followed by litanies of benedictions and blessings, from wishing you peace and good health, to hoping that Allah will facilitate another reunion soon. In whatever little time there is left in the day after greeting and blessing, they (I am mostly talking about men here) spend drinking what I call 'tortured tea,' which I will write about another time. The result is that Malians are some of the most peaceful and at-peace people I have ever met. There is no conflict that cannot be turned to laughter with the right bean-eating joke.

The women indulge just as much in the meeting, greeting, blessing and teasing, but instead of sitting around drinking tea, they clean, wash, cook, raise children, garden, collect firewood, fetch water, and often earn a living too.

Thus the lioness and the joking Coulibaly, Fatumata and Dauda, continue their journey in Mali.

There's No Place Like Home

We are chomping at the bit, but our Regional Coordinator will not show us the house he has picked out for us.

"I want it to look perfect before you see it," he said. "It has a view of the Senegal River from the roof terrace, running water and electricity," he added. "The location is excellent. You can walk to the market, and to the PC Bureau. I know David likes his beer; even the Toubab bar is nearby," he laughs.

This man could sell heaters to the locals on a 115 degree day. Of course he forgot to tell us that the apartment was right on the main road that runs from Bamako to Senegal. We would have a grandstand view of rush hour traffic, as well as the sight and sound show of every semi going past, downshifting to avoid the donkey carts, cyclists and women carrying produce-laden baskets on their heads. Still, we finally get our own place. It was quite disruptive, sharing the bathroom and kitchen with the constant stream of volunteers who popped in and out of the Stage House and who didn't believe in cleaning up after themselves. To have a room of our own was what we wanted so badly. Thus, main road or not, we were quite ready for the next chapter in Lifestyles of the Poor and Ingenious!

We moved into our new apartment: 790 square feet, two bedrooms, two bathrooms and a view, kind of. We have running water, Western-style toilets and electricity – sheer luxury compared to village life. There's cross-ventilation and a fan in every room, and a covered balcony. That's the good news. As for the rest, it's in an old dilapidated building which has been fixed up in the most mickey mouse way – like the plumbing will fall apart if you sneeze. Situation on moving-in day: Turn the light on slightly carelessly, and the switch will pop right out of the wall. Sit on the toilet funny, and the tank will jiggle out of place. A couple of the fans are broken, there are no lights on the stairway, and every time we use the sink it floods the bathroom, whose door doesn't shut. No plumbing at all in the room that will become the kitchen, and the walls are in desperate need of a paint and plaster job. But our regional coordinator assured us that by Malian standards the place was positively pristine. Were D&A phased? Not one bit. Been there, done that many times. We poured ourselves a Pastis, leaned over the balcony to enjoy the river and traffic view, and toasted our new home.

There was a pleasant breeze that first night, and all was right with the world until we went to bed. First a yipping dog nagged us, soon joined by a cacophony of big rigs growling by, screeching, braking, rattling our windows. At one point the sound of a metal door banging had us sitting bolt upright in bed. Has someone broken in already? It happened not once but twice, and the second time I could have sworn I heard footsteps climbing our stairs. The Great White Hunter got up to check it out. Nada. All this would have been not so bad, except that the ambient temperature was well over 100 degrees. Lying under the fan was like sleeping under a giant blow dryer set on high. We were drenched in sweat, as was the bedding; if there had been wild game in the area, they could have used us as a salt lick. Along about midnight David decided to do the wet towel trick (soak a towel in water to cover yourself with, and with the fan going, it cools you down pronto). He went to turn the tap on, and – no water! The water supply pipe had come apart at the street and was spewing like a Vegas fountain on speed. At some point we did manage to fall asleep, only to be awakened at dawn by roosters and the Muslim call to prayer. I was so happy the night was over. With our towels and soap in hand we returned to the Stage House for a shower and shave.

Life at 120 degrees

The fans, the plumbing, the lighting, they all got fixed, at least for a while. The electrician wrapped pieces of plastic grocery bags around the wires in place of electrical tape, not to be outdone by the plumber, who wrapped pieces of the same little plastic bags around pipes to get them to seal. In case you wondered, building codes have yet to be invented here. Our awesome carpenter delivered the kitchen table and shelving right on schedule, though it took a few hours of sanding to make them presentable. Our camping-style three burner gas stove was set up, and the house ghost who tormented our first couple of nights by banging the doors and thumping up the stairs seemed to have given up on us. Before long, we were actually sleeping the night through and life was good, though a little sweaty.

Heat and Dust

On the fifth night in our new abode, we were on our way to dinner when suddenly a wild wind from hell sandblasted us from its reserve supply of sand, the Sahara. We were afraid to open our eyes, and moved forward clutching our clothes, our bags, ourselves, trying hard not to breathe. Our eyes, noses, skins, folds, orifices were all drenched in the fine powder. It blew and it blew, like a whirling dervish gone mad.

 We returned home a couple of hours later during a lull in the storm, to find that indeed the Sahara desert had moved right into our recently cleaned new flat. Half an inch of sand everywhere – on the food, on the stove, on my beautiful new kitchen table. When you have lemons, you make lemonade; does it follow that when you have sand, you build sand castles?

Both of us buckled down and swept and dusted and shook out the sand. We battened down the hatches, and in the still of the night dropped off to sleep under the fan. No need for wet towels that night; the temperature had dropped to a very comfortable 90

Give us this day our daily chores

degrees. Then another crash, bang, slam! Madame Sahara came back even more furiously than before. She raged through the night, and by the time morning came she had exhausted herself – mission accomplished – there was now enough gunk in the air to completely block out the sun. The good news? A positively cool day – a gift after the 112 and 113 degrees we had been having. We dug ourselves out one more time. I have to say that I prefer building my sand castles in the air.

The dust cleared, and the temperature rapidly began to rise like there was no upper speed limit. I had some desperate moments when I was raining sweat and was convinced that my skin had become permanently incontinent; for the rest of my life would I be doomed to carry a super sized, super absorbent bath towel to mop myself? We really couldn't stand in one place for too long, or we'd find ourselves drowning in our very own puddles of gooey sweat, spreading languidly on the floor. The mercury hit 118 degrees for a couple of days this week – definitely a slow bake. Does that mean the Coulibalys will turn into baked beans?

In case you haven't had the pleasure of sleeping in an oven, let me tell you how it is done. Sleep on your back until it is totally basted with sweat. Then turn over on to your side, and feel the coolness of the fan on your wet back (Ooooh, it feels soooo good) until it scorches; then it is time to roll over on your belly. When that is drenched (a few minutes later), roll over onto the other side to cool off. I have felt like a goat rotating on a spit, except this is the reverse of getting evenly roasted – it is about getting evenly cooled off. The thing is, after a few nights your body gets the idea and does it automatically without even waking up, especially if you jump-start the cooling off by covering yourself with a wet *pagne* (sarong) and you are tired enough to fall asleep before the sarong dries out. If the gods are feeling merciful, they will rouse the wind. Better than AC, as long as you don't think about the sand you'll have to breathe or sweep up and shake out the next day. And at the end of it all, you have a good story to tell.

I vow, next hot season we're going to take our entire two-year allotment of vacation time and head for the Moroccan Mediterranean; but for right now, it is back to work and the question of the day: What do I want to do that is worthwhile?

From Despair to Hope

Adama, one of the Assistant Peace Corps Directors (APCD), changed my life. For a Malian man, he is quite Scandinavian in his build – tall and broad-shouldered. He is smart, fluent in English, French and Bambara, and bursting with enthusiasm for his job, his country and the volunteers. Over a beer, I asked him why he loves Peace Corps so much.

Many years ago, he told us, when he was still a young boy, a Peace Corps volunteer used to ride her bike right past his home every day. Every day she waved a hello and rolled on. Adama's dad shook his head: *These foreigners, they are always in a hurry.* One day he could not take any more of this roll-by greeting, so he simply stepped out right in front of her bike, forcing her to swerve to a stop.

"It is very rude how you say hello," he chided.

But if I greeted everybody I see, I would never get to work, she thought but did not say.

The old man insisted she come in and sip sweet tea with him.

There goes the morning, she must have thought. Drinking tea Malian style is a long involved ritual. For myself, I completely understand the volunteer doing ride-by greetings; after all, we are Americans with great deeds to accomplish.

Lurking in the background was this shy young lad, listening in, but keeping his distance as his father and the young lady chatted away. The father made it clear to her that if she wanted to accomplish anything, she must win the hearts and respect of the people; stopping to greet and giving of your time is a good start. This volunteer became a part of the family, and introduced the young boy to the world of books and learning. Adama has never forgotten her, and to this day he insists that if it were not for that rude Peace Corps volunteer with her ride-by hellos, he would not be an APCD today.

In Mali, everyone has time to talk, to drink tea. Everyone is ready to be interested in whatever we have to say. Yet as soon as the conversation turns to "Let us do something about it," there is

SILENCE, a very awkward silence. This happens every day at the health center. *Moringa is a great idea, but you want me to do what? I am too busy, can't you see it is tea time already?* But not Adama, he is a doer. He renewed my sense of hope about making a difference.

With Adama I floated ideas about starting a small hand-made paper co-op, and possibly a small business of quilt making from all the fabulous cloth remnants that get tossed out at the thousands of tailor shops around town. The next day he set up an appointment with Madame Denbele. She is one very flamboyant, effervescent woman, who drives around Kayes in an orange Humvee. As the executive director of Muso Danbe (Women with Dignity), a non-profit, she is hell-bent on helping women help themselves. She provides them with training for new skills, organizes them into cooperatives, helps market the products they make, and much more. She's ambitious; she's tireless, she's absolutely charming, and what's more, she said she would love to see how I could help.

Madame Denbele, wife of a professor, mother of six, recognized a long time ago that women needed professions too, other than as sex workers. She started in a small way, teaching orphans and handicapped girls what she knew – how to make *bazan*. Bazan is the nicest cloth in Mali. It's a shiny, waxy, hand dyed fabric that Malians wear for the finest occasions, such as weddings and the big Muslim holidays, or for meeting important guests. She marketed what the orphans made and, with success building upon success, went wild with what ifs – all the possibilities for cast-out women to create new lives. She became a regular on the bus to Bamako, seeking out anyone with power or money to support her plans. With charm, enthusiasm and energy it was not long before she became every donor's sweetheart, and for good reason. Denbele delivered. She built a grassroots training center in Kayes, which is where I came to make my pitch to her. Within minutes she interrupted me to pull some of her staff and students into the meeting. Before I knew it, I was enlisted to teach several classes to add to her success story:

From 1999 to 2008 at Muso Danbe,

- *698 women were trained in dyeing*
- *549 women in soap making*
- *40 in dressmaking*
- *329 in recycling*
- *99 in hand embroidery*
- *25 in weaving*
- *15 in machine embroidery*
- *204 women made literate, and*
- *2103 informed and sensitized about circumcision, STD / AIDS, hygiene, sanitation, health and life skills.*

I'm in business working with the most dynamic woman I have ever met in Mali! I've been on a high ever since. I don't have to have my heart broken all day weighing listless bony ghost babies to (maybe) save them from dying! I would probably earn more Mother Theresa points for the latter, but my energy truly belongs in the more creative world of crafts and business. What I am going to tell the doctor about jumping ship, I'm not quite sure. Better a happy quilt marketer than a baby weigher with an attitude.

If that wasn't enough happiness, a few early rains have had me wanting to run out naked into the street, to dance wildly and catch those precious droplets in my mouth. In this regard I have shown tremendous restraint, for which I do hope I earn a medal.

These rains have been extremely satisfying. Thunder claps, whirlwinds, lightening shows and powerful downpours that entice you to come out and watch. Like good guests, the squalls don't hang around too long. They do their thing and move on, leaving behind sweet smells and mud and even more mud. Hey, I could start up a mud bath spa.

The temperatures are closer to 100 now, and dropping. Life is worth living. I love Peace Corps. I love Mali!

So Sue Me!

Our neighbor, Appui Amader's Atelier de Production de Fourneau, the metal works, provides us with a non-stop cacophony of bangs, bonks, tocks, whacks and crashes. It is a major junkyard of rusting rail road ties, gutted trucks, severely disabled wheel barrows, bent out of shape metal drums, and heaps and heaps of discarded, rusty, mean-looking metal doodads strewn everywhere, just waiting to slice up an unsuspecting child. Not a single lawsuit has ever brought into question the safety of this operation. No laws! No lawyers, despite the fact that death traps abound.

When I first gingerly ventured into this graveyard of hidden treasures and sharp shards of metal, the bells of fear rang in my head. Tetanus, lockjaw and slow painful death were just one wrong step away. I was looking for something sharp, pointy and small to carve designs into wood, to make embossing stamps for my paper making project.

I tippy-toed around looking for the perfect shard, attracting a gaggle of barefoot kids who ran around as though it were a beach of soft sand. "Toubab! Toubab!" they hailed. They were not going to miss the opportunity of shaking my hand, or asking for a *cadeau*. Guessing by their ages (really young) they probably had no clue what a cadeau was (it's French for gift), but that is what kids do when a Toubab materializes. I was the circus freak, the source of endless entertainment. Suddenly I had helpers. They had no clue about what it was I was looking for, but now they were each picking up random pieces for my approval even as I was freaking out about their feet being shredded to bits. My frenzy totally paralyzed me when I saw a metal worker swinging a 20 pound hammer; it clanked down within two inches of the fingers that were holding down the metal. They use humans as clamps! No goggles, no gloves, no fire-retardant materials to protect them from the fountain of sparks erupting all around. Kids, animals, and whoever else wanted, wandered around the workshop as though they were strolling in the park.

I did find suitable carving tools for my project. They resembled museum finds from a stone-age excavation site. It was totally appropriate for my cave-person existence here in Mali. Okay, so I am a cave person with running water and electricity. What kind of cave person would you want to be? I did my first carving of a mother breast-feeding her child. The tools worked. Unfortunately, these handle-less tools triggered a mega-inflammation in my right thumb. Years of weeding in Hawaii had overworked the thumb joint and caused a severe depletion of Ibuprofen in my body. I am sure you all know that arthritis is a Vitamin I deficiency disease!

But that is not what I wanted to write about. I want to write about just how unsafe this whole country is when viewed through American eyes – and I don't mean war or crime or anything

Embossing template

heinous stemming from ill intentions. Mali would be declared a disaster by the EPA, EEO, OSHA, and any other safety-and-rights-ensuring-agency. The whole country is one enormous building code violation; by American laws, it would be cordoned off by and with yellow tape, patrolled by the National Guard and declared unsafe for human habitation. Nobody, but nobody would be allowed entry, let alone permission to live here. This is a place where every child has an extremely high probability of breaking their legs, poking their eyes out, and catching pneumonia, ten times a day every day. Yet it is not those proverbial fatalities that kill the kids – just untreated malaria and malnutrition.

What is truly amazing is how well this country does function, despite the lack of governance, law enforcement, industry safety standards or watchdogs. People have the freedom to earn a living in any way they can (safe or unsafe), and without being liable, yet victims are few and far between. If one gets diarrhea from street food, you just cope with it, for it too shall pass... so to speak. If someone sets up a mini-kiosk next to your front door to sell tea and sugar, you accept it unless it is totally in your way. The give and take, the collaboration to make their society work and tolerate huge inconveniences is taken for granted. Of course poverty and the lack of infrastructure do not attract the Walmarts and McDonalds, so an economy at the tiny scale is free to flourish.

Taxis are often vehicles that should have been junked ten years ago, with cracked windshields, bashed-in chassis, and engines being held together with a prayer and strips of plastic bags. The keys to the ignition have long been lost. In fact, there *is* no ignition, or a working battery. Hot wiring and jump-starting is how these wrecks are made to move. They cram nine people inside, plus a roof rack full of luggage and sacks of rice and millet to transport medium to long distances. When they break down, which they often do – oh well, you are out of your fare. You either hitchhike the rest of the way, or wait patiently for the guy to jury-rig a fix. No Triple A, no rescue taxi, just another piece of what you have to accept and cope with. Having said that, so far, for the number of times (a lot) I have had to ride these cabs, only twice was I left stranded, and then not for very long. The second time, when the transmission gave out the driver simply flagged down a truck. All eleven passengers clambered on top of its seven tons of onion sacks, and we had a most scenic and perfumed ride to our destination. No complaining, no bitching, no entitlement. Passengers simply accept and go with the program, and so did we.

From functional taxi wrecks to street food spiced with road dirt and truck fumes, there is a huge informal economy. Very few people have permits. No one buys liability insurance, even if there were any to be had. There are no certified kitchens or inspectors.

This informal economy may sound chaotic, but with people free to earn a dime or two in whatever way they can, there is an incredible range of services available. You have a whetstone? Hook it up to your bike to earn a few dimes sharpening knives and anything else that needs sharpening. When David's almost new Teva sandals tore and would have been landfill at home, the cobbler who sets up on the sidewalk in front of the bank pulled out caveman implements from his magic bag and voila! He added another year to the life of the sandals. You have a sewing machine? Mount it on the back of your bike and ride around town to see if anybody needs some mending done. Then there is the enchanting little girl who sets up outside of our front door, selling small bags of salted peanuts on the street; she melts David's heart and he regularly buys her whole stock, setting him back a good 50 cents or so. It reminds us of American kids and their lemonade stands, except, for this little girl, the money surely goes to supporting her family.

As there are no regulation setbacks or required numbers of parking spots, corner shops and makeshift kiosks abound, selling sugar and tea, and little sachets of washing powder. Public transport to the surrounding villages is plentiful, provided by the people and for the people who have loads of time but little money. Comfort is not of the essence – just be happy to be getting a cheap ride. In a country where the job market doesn't really exist, people earn a living every which way they can. In fact many of our volunteers work with locals in the informal sector, teaching them illiterate accounting skills (how to document and track their income and expenses using images), as well as basic market research. They show them ways to add value to their products. In its own way, that is David's mandate at the CMC.

Despite – or more likely because of – the lack of regulation and anything that resembles enforceable safety standards, and because of the lack of universal health care, social security, unemployment insurance and countless other safety nets, the responsibility for staying alive, alert, nimble and out of harm's way belongs entirely to the individual and the family. I love that aspect of the Malian value system. Death is not a failure to survive, but an accepted part of life; many people die, but seldom because of the lack of safety enforcers. Sixty-three percent of all deaths in Mali are attributed to malaria… a very different story.

Don't get me wrong, I am not advocating abolishing laws and taxes and civil rights. They are very important. I love that in the States, I neither have to breathe the fumes of burning plastic garbage, nor do I have to tolerate stinky clogged up open sewers, or be discriminated against because of my sex or race. However, the culture of entitlement, so prevalent in our country, is giving it a reputation of being a country full of victims, and that is something that should be challenged. How much insurance do we really need? Are we willing to take no risks at all as far as safety is concerned, so that the cost of providing services becomes unaffordably high? Malians, in contrast, completely accept that shit happens all the time, and that you have to make the most of life the best way you can. Indeed this is a very gracious, generous and civilized culture – as long as we don't talk about female genital mutilation and a few other things like that.

I wonder where Americans would be without some their laws and rights, and where Malian would be if they had a few more of the same.

Reflections

You can never be just yourself in a foreign country where you cannot speak the language well enough to explain who you are. You become a label. In Mali I am a Toubab. I am burdened with whatever deeds or misdeeds my predecessors may have committed.

"....but you are a Toubab, you must be rich, you must be able to get us an American visa," they say.

In my broken Bambara, I try to explain that the American Embassy does not work that way, but they do not believe me.

Instead my answer reinforces the common knowledge that *Toubabs really don't care about us, and they do not share their wealth.* Whatever I do or say is fitted into that Toubab label.

Not really knowing Malian values and beliefs, I suppose I do the same in order to make sense of the bizarre, like female genital mutilation. That would fit very neatly under the label *barbarians* or *backward.* In desperate moments, when I simply don't get where the Malians are coming from, and when I see the immensity of the problems here – which go beyond the rampant hunger for food and for jobs – I wonder with my American brain and eyes whether Mali truly is a basket case, and the little drop of salve that I bring will just get lost in the sands of the Sahara.

But with at least one person, my Bambara teacher Moussa, both he and I are burning the labels we have for each other, to see the real people behind them and, possibly, unconsciously redefining the labels.

Moussa, is an educated and responsible family man. He teaches accounting at the junior college and wants so badly to open his own school of accounting.

"Why?" I ask, thinking government jobs are secure and well paid.

"It is better when I collect the fees," he says. "I don't have to worry about money."

He tells me that he and all the teachers have not been paid for several months now. Neither have the police, but they can collect their paychecks directly from the people by setting up road blocks. If any of your driver's paperwork is out of order, for a small price the cops will let you go. However, if you stand on principle and refuse to pay the bribe, you will get strangled by a basket-load of red tape to sort out the ticket you just acquired. As Moussa tells me this, now I begin to understand why the road blocks, and to see the ingenuity of people in the face of adversity, doing just what they have to do to survive.

"Moussa, how many children do you have?" I ask.

"Only three boys. I want more, but my wife, she does not want."

"Moussa, do you know how many children most Americans have?"

He shakes his head.

"Not more than two or three," I tell him. "That is why they are rich."

The last sentence gets his attention.

"How can they be rich with so few children?" He is quite puzzled.

"Because with just two children, they can afford medicine when the children are sick. The children do not die. Also they can save money to send their children to University, so that they can earn more money."

He takes in the information but does not say anything.

"How many children do you and Dauda have?" he asks.

"None," I say with enthusiasm.

"I am so sorry. I will pray that Allah will bless you."

At fifty seven that would be a biblical miracle, I think, but instead I say,

"You don't understand, Moussa, Dauda and I decided not to have children."

"What! You cannot decide that." He thinks I am mad. Toubabs have strange ideas. They dare to go against the natural order. "But who will look after you when you are old?"

"You and your children will!" I say. "All the world's children are my children, that is why I came to volunteer in Mali, to make children's lives better."

I had memorized that line, as indeed it came up often, and that was the most comprehensible and noble answer I could give. He laughed and said I am very welcome. I can stay with his family and he will build me my own room in his compound. I have absolutely no doubt that he would.

At Moussa's

It was exactly these small conversations that shredded the labels. To him I was no longer *Toubab* but *my sister Fatumata*, and to me he went from being a typical Malian Male to a very dear friend and younger brother. Moussa adopted David and me. Every Sunday we would bicycle to his house on the other side of the river, where he would spend far too much on buying meat and sodas for us. After lunch I would nap on the piece of foam under the tree with his sister, aunt and wife until it was time to sip at least three cups of very sweet tea. Then I would bring out my deck of UNO cards. It was as exciting playing with them as it was going to a cock fight. A crowd would materialize around us, cheering at every 'take four,' discussing our hands like we had a million dollars at stake; they would hold their breaths when someone shouted out with gusto UNO! and burst into raucous applause when someone won. The audience could not wait for their turn to join the game. And thus we slowly slotted into Malian lives.

Of course, each new arrival always asked how many children we had. Immediately Moussa would jump in and explain to them that we chose not to have children, and that in America they purposely have fewer children and that is why they are rich! Progress.

Most Malians have nothing, but they live as though their bellies, their hearts, their souls are filled with abundance. It is only our eyes that see the swollen pot belly of a child and know that it comes from a lack of food. It is only our eyes that see women without any rights, slaving away in the fields and in their compounds. It is only our eyes that measure their lacks. Yet I see that their glass is also half full. They can completely count on each other and their children, their nieces and nephews, to see them through hard times. They are each other's care givers, each other's social security, and each other's guardians. 'My house is your house' is practiced without it ever being said. Part of their greeting when an outsider arrives is "You have left home, but you have come home."

At some level I know I have come home, and this is what keeps me ticking as I slowly surrender my Western ways and enjoy this roller coaster. I get excited when the shower actually works – which it does, as long as you don't sneeze. If you do, the head will fall off again. The funny thing was, after a while I found David using little pieces of plastic bag to secure the shower head back in place! In Mali I remember that life is about how we touch each other; and right now, we are being touched a lot. Every cell in my body celebrates the smile I receive or the excitement when a kid runs alongside me calling,

"Toubab, Toubab, donne moi cadeau."

"No, I say. You give a _me_ a gift."

One time the kid gave me his 10 cent coin. Mostly the kids are bursting with curiosity and just want to play. Getting me to do High Fives with them sends them into fits of giggles, like they scored something really big. How can I not slow down and breathe in their silliness, their excitement, their laughter. These are the moments that take my breath away, and there is a bouquet full of these moments, waiting to be delivered every day. How can I not fall in love with my life in this dusty town on the edge of the Sahara? Indeed, I had not bargained for a love affair with life, but that is what I got in coming to Mali as a Peace Corps volunteer.

Food – Which Do I Prefer, Sex or Chocolate?

> *Toubab shop has Nutella*, a volunteer just texted me.

Before I could be transported to that ecstatic place where I could stick my fingers straight into the jar and slowly lick every last molecule of creamy hazelnut chocolate from my fingers, I had to fly to the bank to get some cash and then tear to the store to claim one of the jars, assuming there was one left on the shelf. Would I make it in time? Yesssss!

Ahhhh, the heightened joys of deprivation! I never truly appreciated just how much I took for granted. The refrigerator door doodad that automatically pumps iced water into a glass is a wet dream from long ago. Here in Kayes, warm water from our filter is all we get. The Stage House freezer (the tiny compartment above the fridge) is filled with plastic bottles, frozen solid. We bring one home whenever we can and, as the ice melts (very quickly), each sip is champagne from the best vintner.

Eat whatever is available locally, has always been my policy when traveling or living abroad; but going months without chocolate, that is reason enough to stage a revolution. Devoured by desire for anything chocolate, I tried the local stuff, only to realize that chocolate was a color, not a flavor, in Mali. "I have self control; I have will power; I am virtuous and therefore I can live without chocolate," I say to myself every day.

I rushed out of the house equally fast when my phone bleeped with the message *>green beans at market*. I bought far more than what we could eat, but what the hell, who knows when I will see them next. Enough said about chocolate and green beans.

The big question still remains, how am I going to cook the cabbage today – truly a cruciferous culinary conundrum. How I wish I could be like the Malians and eat white rice and mystery sauce day in and day out – and consider myself blessed that I have anything to eat at all. The sauce is a mystery because the ingredients, usually tomatoes, garlic, and whatever else they found or grew, is crushed to a homogenous paste and then cooked to a point where there is no discernible flavor of any individual ingredient. Sometimes the sauce is red, sometimes green (and slimy, if it is made with okra). My personal favorite is brown sauce – the peanut butter sauce.

Shopping for food is not about going to the local climate-controlled supermarket and filling up the trolley – no trolleys, no supermarkets. It is threading your way through the crowded market, from the tomato lady to the potato man to the mango seller, greeting each one, telling the required bean jokes, checking the wares, bargaining, paying, and moving onto the next vendor for the next item. The ingredients gathered, I can only cook for one meal, or else we'll be eating bacteria pie.

For twenty eight days in a row, all they have had at the market is cabbage, tomatoes, eggplant, green peppers and okra. Most likely it will be the same cast of characters for the next twenty eight. Cabbage, eggplant and green pepper soup again? I take my stipend and go to the Toubab shop to buy little plastic cheese triangles of La Vache Qui Rit (the laughing cow), cans of mackerel in tomato sauce, and some spaghetti.

We cook for ourselves. In an effort to eat healthily, Experimental Food Science is alive and well in our kitchen. A three-burner camping stove sits at one end of the eight-foot kitchen table and counter, and the five gallon bucket that is our water filter sits at the other end. We have no refrigerator, no microwave, no blender, no nothing. I am the proud inventor of the okra-stuffed omelet, and make a mean canned mackerel and cabbage spaghetti sauce, loaded with garlic and fried onions. Even so, day after day of cabbage and or okra or eggplant does make me gag.

Eating local food really does not take much courage. It is not like when we were in China. There they served deep-fried scorpion that I had to pick up with my chopsticks, its eyes looking straight into mine and saying "just you dare..." But I had to, because my hosts were waiting on me to take that first bite. I drew the line when they brought live snakes in – I simply fled the restaurant. For the first time ever, even a McDonalds hamburger sounded appetizing. The only scary part about Malian food is the fly-covered meat, sitting in blobs or hanging off hooks at the meat market. I don't buy meat. Thus it is canned mackerel again for dinner. Once a week, we eat out.

The best part about living in a regional capital that is also a major truck stop hub: small eateries observing many different levels of hygiene abound. You decide how many flies you would like to have as a side! We have pastry shops, hamburger and brochette places, and one very fancy pizza place, delightfully set on the terrace by the pool with bougainvillea cascading from the walls, at our only (self-proclaimed) three star hotel. Since we have to take out a second mortgage to eat and swim there, we reserve it for very special occasions.

My favorites are the street food vendors. Anywhere and everywhere, ladies set up their little coal stoves with huge wok-like frying pans, in which they deep fry little rice or millet-flour fritters and then roll them in sugar. Others fry fish to a crisp and sell small bits of them in sandwiches made from fluffy baguettes. A few women, like Mme. Fanta, precook enormous cauldrons of meat sauce, beans and macaroni. Fanta sets up her table made of distressed planks and bricks, and throws a *pangne* cloth over it. We crowd around her with a dozen other customers, holding our plates and waiting our turn. When she catches my eye a hush falls, as other clients strain to hear what this Toubab will buy, and then burst into surprised chatter as they hear Bambara words fall out of my mouth;

"Fifty cents of salad, $1 of meat, 50 cents of macaroni," is what I tell her, handing her my plate. She piles the salad on, but then fishes out from her cauldron the exact number of bite-size pieces of meat that I had paid for. Every once in a while she throws in an extra.

Cooking local food is truly a challenge, since the raw ingredients are really raw! One cannot just go out and buy millet flour or rice flour. You have to buy the millet and clean it, removing the stones, the sand, and whatever else that thought the millet sack was a good place to live and raise a family. After the physical clean, it must be washed and left in the sun to dry. It is now ready

The Frufru Lady

to be pounded into flour, which in turn must be winnowed to remove the chaff from the flour. I asked one of the women to prepare millet flour for me. My mouth watered at the thought of making unleavened bread, just the way my mom used to, with loads of crushed garlic, a liberal sprinkle of pepper, some chilies, and a few precious pinches of cumin, coriander and turmeric that I had brought from home. I used only a little of the millet flour and made the bread. Ohhh so good. I saved the rest for another day. Not even two days later, furry mold robbed me of my precious flour.

From joy to disappointment, like a yoyo I would swing. I'd console myself with the thought that it was not going to be long before we have to go to Bamako for work. Down there is the Biiiig Toubab shop, where expats and the uber-rich Malians shop. It's the closest thing Mali has to our supermarkets at home. As we cruise down the aisles, we are like kids on Christmas morning, ripping open gifts, looking for surprises. Oh look, they have lentils and chick peas and… oh my goodness, look, they have Tahini! Who would have thought.

It is totally random what appears on the shelves; it's entirely a matter being at the right place at the right time to score a packet of Oreos or muesli. Last time I found a jewel-sized bottle of balsamic vinegar. We won't talk about how much it cost, and I have no clue how the mostly-Lebanese shop owners obtain their goods. When we returned to Kayes we got a huge break from eating cabbage soup. I made hummus, and invited all the local volunteers. We ate and enjoyed it in the same way as one would Thanksgiving dinner – including the giving of thanks.

Rain or Hunger

I don't think we have ever spent so much of our lives cleaning house as we have done here. Yes, the rain finally came on August 16. It blew in through the closed windows, seeped under the door, and in some places mysterious puddles appeared just because they could. The night of the first major storm, we were so happy that we didn't even notice being marooned on our bed as the tide rose on the apartment floor. If it had rained any more, we would be paddling through the apartment with a serving spoon as an oar and our large Teflon wok as a raft. Okay, so it was not as bad as that, but while it did take the two of us a good couple of hours to mop up the mess, it was a welcome chore.

How I love the rain for turning on Nature's own air conditioning. Goodbye 120 degrees, welcome mud puddles – and mosquitoes, and having to do battle with the armies of kamakazi bugs that die

gloriously in our food, our bed, and indeed on our toilet paper.
Even though our apartment is mostly screened in, somehow
mites and bites are still the irritating order of the day. Normally it
is a lot worse, I am told. By now it should be pouring every day
for about six to eight weeks. Not this year. Dark clouds roll in
and the winds howl and whistle, sending anybody and everybody
on the streets scurrying for shelter. A few drops of rain accidently
get blown our way and raise our hopes. Then suddenly it is all
over. The clouds go bye-bye, the wind drops, and another day of
no rain comes and goes. If the situation does not change soon, I
may be writing a very different epistle about what we are eating.
Fewer bugs but...... poor farmers!

Rain or no rain, Hunger Season is upon Mali. It is the time period
from when the grain harvested from the previous year runs out,
to when the new harvest comes in. Sometimes Hunger Season is
very short, but this year my friend Ousmane, who sits in the tiny
alleyway between our building and the next, selling gourd bowls,
says people have already run out of food. There is at least two to
three months to go before the next harvest.

"What happens to them?"

"They must buy food, he tells me," but already prices are high."

"Do you have enough food at home?"

"Allah will provide. He is merciful."

Does that mean Ousmane has food, or is he hoping that
somebody will buy one of his gourds today so that he can take
home a little bit of rice? My African-children-are-starving
heartstrings are being tugged at.

Ousmane and I regularly drink three cups of tea together, in the alleyway. It is always three cups, which are not really cups but are shot glasses of bitter sweet tea, for that is the custom. As we sit he tells me stories, like the one about how afraid Malians are of cats.

"But they are so cute. In America we keep them as pets and treat them like our own children," I tell him.

With terror in his eyes, he says that in Mali cats jump at your throat and drink your blood.

Wow. Vampire cats.

"Have you seen them do that?"

"No, but I don't like cats. I kill them before they can kill me."

That explains why I saw kids dangling a kitten from the end of a string, torturing the poor thing.

"Just stop!" I yelled. But before I could do anything, the kids and the dangling kitty were gone, over the walls and into the alleys. An amused passerby stopped. I was still shaking with rage.

"It is okay, he said, "the boys need the food."

The words did not begin to comfort me, but then what do I know about being hungry day after day? My heart was still with the kitty.

The boys deserve to starve, was the thought I didn't share.

Today Ousmane didn't pull out his little metal teapot.

"You are not having tea today?"

78

"I don't feel like it," he says.

I knew then that he didn't have a nickel in his pocket for tea and sugar.

"Would you make me some?" I ask, giving him a couple of match-box sized packets of green tea, a small bag of sugar and a few lumps of coal. He fires up the little stove, and in his much used metal teapot boils the water with the tea in it. It will take an hour at least, so I settle down on the ground on his frayed mat.

"No no," he says and runs across the street to borrow a chair from the carpenter. He lets the tea and the water boil. I ask him about his family as he washes the three shot glasses that will be our tea cups. He fills one of the glasses to the brim with sugar, then he remembers.

"Fatumata, doesn't like sugar," he says to the two other men who have materialized and have made themselves comfortable on his fraying mat. I suspect that they, like Ousmane, left their homes right after first prayer, without eating breakfast, so that there would be more food to go around for the family. Now that this Toubabu has bought tea and sugar, a small blessing from Allah, they joined in.

"No, I will have sugar today," I insist.

He pours it into the teapot and lets it boil a lot more. The shorter of two other guys tells me how he has not eaten for days... Ousmane breaks in, embarrassed that his friend is brazenly begging.

"Fatumata ye Corps de la Paix wolɔntɛri ye."

"But they must pay her," the friend insists. "She is a Toubabu."

Ousmane now fills one of the glasses with the tea from the pot by pouring it from a low height, then raising the teapot as high as he can before bringing it low again. When the glass is full, he pours it back into the teapot with a flick of the wrist. He repeats, and repeats, and repeats the process until the glass has a good head of froth.

Making the tea is a ponderous, plodding process that simply cannot be rushed. I hate the sickly sweet and bitter flavor, but I love the time it takes to make it. I love the banter and chat as he tortures the tea. We talk about birth control, his young wife, about Moringa, his travels to neighboring Senegal. Today we have company, and much of his time is taken with calming the visitors and keeping them from hounding me to rescue their miserable lives. I love Ousmane. It was his wife who made the millet flour for me.

Finally he takes a small sip and, deciding the tea is just right, offers me the first glass. I pass it on to the visitors after a tiny sip that makes my mouth pucker and cringe. Horrible stuff! They all laugh.

"Fatumata does not like your tea. You must buy her Lipeeton." (That is Lipton tea bag tea!) I am grateful that the conversation has taken a turn, but do not stay for the second and third round where the whole process is repeated, reusing the same leaves.

At the market I pick up some fish and fruit and give it to Ousmane.

"It is for your children," I say. He is so embarrassed. His proud, sharply sculpted face had tried to hide the hunger. Now it looks defeated.

"May Allah bless you."

"Amina!" I say but feel like I crossed an invisible line. I very awkwardly ask for the road (say goodbye) and head on home. I have made him feel bad, and that bothers me.

I wonder what it would have felt like if our roles were reversed. What if I was the hungry one and hadn't earned a penny to help feed my family, let alone myself. What would it feel like if some wealthy friend gave me some fish and fruit? Wouldn't I be grateful? Yes, but now I can see how my gratitude would be tinged with shame – shame because I received charity from a friend. Is that what Ousmane was feeling? Will our friendship change because of an action I hadn't thought through?

The old adage of teaching a person to fish just does not apply here. When the rain does not come, there is no food in the Sahel. These people have endured many famines, but does that make it any easier going through one more? Do you ever get used to being hungry and watching your children die because of the lack of food? No! No! No! the voice from inside of me said.

I had lost my appetite for supper that night. I went to bed without eating, and started praying for rain. Each time the wind came up, my hopes soared. With the rest of the farmers, I was willing the clouds to bring rain and dump it on us.

"Come on, come on, pleeease come and rain on us. I really love cleaning my floors!"

Back home in Hawaii we get 120 inches a year. Dear God, can't you spread out these precious resources a little better? If God cannot, then how powerful am I? There really isn't any divine justice is there – only how you cope with both the good times and the desperate times.

Ousmane's friends coped by begging, pulling guilt trips on the Toubab. Ousmane coped more quietly. He counted his blessings wherever he could and trusted that Allah knows best. And I? I went out and bought food for my friend in need and came home, brooding and looking for answers. Would there have been less shame had I had bought a couple of his calabashes instead?

The good thing about life is that there are loads of opportunities to learn how to do it differently the next time. This time all I could do was to buy fruit and fish, but next time... Next time I will take a deep breath or two to still my mind, so that I can hear the quiet voice of the soul that is much wiser than my clever mind. Maybe over future cups of tea, Ousmane and I can brainstorm ideas about how to provide for the next hunger season.

Today I gave thanks, for it rained. I pray that it does so tomorrow and the many morrows after that.

Here Comes the Moringa Queen

Oh my God, it is almost the end of August; Time, please wait for me. I am falling behind and it will soon be time to go home and... and... and... I am not quite ready yet, at least not this week. Three months ago I could not even begin to imagine that I would feel this way.

What changed? I finally stopped feeling guilty (well, not completely) about all that I ought to be doing at the clinic, and started to do things that I love. I have just finished teaching a papermaking workshop to a bunch of mynah birds at Muso Danbe. At the beginning they were terribly quiet, reverential, almost pretending not to be there, while keeping a sharp eye on me. How I wished then they would talk, or laugh. I am not a prison warden, I wanted to say, but the word for prison warden in Bambara eluded me. By the end of class the girls chattered and screeched, and giggled and teased – but oh so loudly that I longed for that reverential quiet. "Mudum, mudum, mudum!" fell out of their mouths like yippy pups, as they snapped their fingers in the air simultaneously to catch Madame Asifa's attention. If I looked at them sternly and asked them to wait their turn, it bought me a 10 second reprieve before the finger snapping and Mudum tape restarted.

What fun it was to get back to doing something that remotely resembles art and creativity, and while my gaggle of 17 year olds had fun too, teaching them was like a game of Simon Says. They do their damndest to ape what Mudum does. When I finally respond to their mudums and finger snapping, what do I hear – "Is this right? Is this good? Is this like yours?"

Paper-making class

I have been doing wood cuts and carving gourds – trying to create something different that may sell. What if Ousmane spent some of his many hours of just sitting and waiting, carving simple designs on his gourds? Would they sell better, or fetch a higher price? As it is, he is one of several vendors selling exactly the same thing in the same market. Before I could complete a couple of samples, the carving had to stop. The ham of my right thumb started hurting more than ever, so much so, I had to call Dr. Dawn. I could not do anything with my right hand.

"Take Ibuprofen thee times daily and do absolutely nothing for five days" were the good Doctor's orders. I miss chopping onions, scrubbing floors and hand-washing clothes like I miss walking barefoot on ice. Saint David has lived up to his name. For the moment he is doing it all – the scrubbing, washing and chopping.

What else was there but to let my brain think, as I sat around without any chores to do. The five little words that my husband has come to dread – *Honey, I have been thinking.....* This time it did not involve moving furniture or moving houses or countries. In fact it did not involve moving or him at all. My I-have-been-thinking was for the Food Security Group. It occurred to me that if we helped every health center in the country grow and dispense dried Moringa leaves and seedlings, it might have a real effect on reducing malnutrition. I typed up a brief outline for a plan to do such a project, and sent it off to Peace Corps' Food Security Group. Well what do you know – the powers that be thought it was a great idea, "And by the way, we unanimously voted for you to head up this initiative." Oops. I guess I am going to be a little busy for the next few weeks.

My task was to put together a Moringa kit that not only contained a more organized *all-you-ever-wanted-to-know-about-Moringa-but-were-afraid-to-ask* manual, but also a step by step, month by month training package for the volunteers on how to implement the project in their villages. I had to design presentations to be used in places where there is no power (therefore no PowerPoint), and where people are not literate (therefore no handouts). I included scripts for radio shows in several indigenous languages, a portfolio of drawings that village volunteers could use to paint murals, as well as a recipe book for how to cook with Moringa. My deadline? Halloween, just two months away. The Moringa training would begin with the new group of volunteers who would be landing in Bamako then.

Moringa mural at Tubaniso

Hurray, I get to work in English and tap into the trainer in me. Immediately I began making checklists:

Rally up support from the Peace Corps staff from other disciplines (Ag, environment, small business and education); identify various governmental and non-governmental health organizations to partner with in this project; create a team of volunteers to help make the project a reality; and so on. I loved it. I loved working from my strength rather than my weakness. I am arrogant enough to think that if I try hard enough, I can do just about anything. Trying to gain some fluency in Bambara was one of my failures, and the single biggest source of bellyache, heartache and headache. Reluctantly, I conceded defeat and decided to move on. The result? A happier Asifa.

I Am Too Old for This!

With the Moringa project began many trips to Bamako, which meant staying at the infamous Bamako Stage House – the living quarters PC provides for volunteers who come to Bamako on business. There are four double-decker bunk beds per bedroom, and three bathrooms that 24 of us share when the house is full, which it almost always is. Physically it is a lovely single family house, gracious and spacious, well suited to those who have delusions of grandeur. In its present incarnation, the feel is more like a frat house the day after a big football game. The place is strewn with dirty dishes, with uneaten morsels of congealed food on plates, pans, tables and floor. Rucksacks are piled high, and laundry sits in puddles on whatever leftover floor space there is. The bathrooms are permanently wet. Two dozen 20-something year olds with raging hormones are languidly draped over the furniture, unwashed feet on the coffee tables, nursing their laptops, their Iphones and hangovers simultaneously. They like their TV loud, and would watch an entire season of *Jersey Shore* in one sitting, just because they could. I totally don't get why otherwise very smart and accomplished kids would watch such an asinine show.

"It makes us feel superior," said one of them.

I wonder. Nice kids individually, but a pack of them with no parents around? That is a little more stimulation than I am used to.

I was so happy to return home to Kayes, even if four days later I had to turn around and take the redeye back to Bamako. For better or for worse, I have several more trips to the capital. The new group of volunteers arrives on October 30 and I have been designated the special trainer for the Moringa project, which means I'll be spending a lot of time at the Training Center and in Bamako in the coming months.

If I Had Only a Year To Live, I Would…

After weeks of 12 hour days and commuting to Bamako, my brain and body have downshifted – no, actually they have slipped into idle. All my brain would let me do is to check e-mail, Facebook and Google News. Steve Jobs had died, and I clicked on the URL to re-listen to the commencement speech he gave at Stanford a few years back. Sitting here in Kayes Mali, I had to ask myself the same question that he had been in the habit of asking himself.

"If today were the last day of my life, is *this* what I would want to be doing?" The quiet answer from within was *Yes*. How about, if I knew this were the last year of my life, would I choose to continue to serve with Peace Corps, Mali? I had to think about that one.

Very little about living here is comfortable, what with the heat, the bugs, the sameness of the food, the polluted air we breathe, and the pug-ugly dusty landscape. Would I jump ship if I knew I only had a year more to live? I surprised myself. The answer was no, I would not. I hate being vulnerable, but I love the soft and more authentic side vulnerability brings out in me. Despite the discomfort and challenges, I am very engaged with life, trying to make it work and trying to make something out of it. Having been stripped of all luxury for nine months now, I have become so easy to please. The smallest things, like a flower or a smile, leave me with a deep sense of gratitude and pleasure. The laughter of the children and the people here delight more than any Christmas gift I have ever opened. I love not knowing what tomorrow holds. I love that control is something I lack over here – well, sometimes.

The Moringa project is progressing. Many of the responsibilities have been delegated, which has now freed me up to work on 'Project Design and Management' in the context of development. I was quite critical of the way these sessions were presented to our group, and told them so in my evaluation. The Director of Training called and asked if I would help redo the course.

"Would love to!" was my instant answer.

Now that I actually have to come up with a proposal for the sessions, I find I am a little out of my depth, not that that has stopped me in the past. The first thing I did was to try and define what development was in the Malian context. Here are some musings.

300 Cups of Tea

Under the gracious shade of a Neem tree, I was having tea with Moussa and his fellow teachers at the community college. They were on strike for not having been paid for many months now. They still came to work, but instead of teaching, they sat under the tree, making and sipping tea, talking story. I was the only woman sharing their tea.

"Where are the other women?"

"At home."

"How come the women teachers don't sit around and drink tea?"

"They have much work to do at home." They boasted.

"So why aren't you at home helping?"

This provoked much laughter and talking amongst themselves that alluded to the silliness of my suggestion. I sat there like a school teacher waiting for an answer, and then called on Sidi, a young man who was thoroughly enjoying being in the company of this older American woman. He even spoke some English, very advanced for Kayes. I could see him puff up like peacock to correct my ignorance.

"Our women tell us to go away. They don't want our help."

"Of course they don't want a bunch of lazy layabouts hanging around making a nuisance of themselves, asking them to do this and that. American women would kick you out of the house too." They laughed in recognition of the picture of them I had just painted.

They love hearing about life in America and found it hilarious that my husband, a University professor, would do the laundry and wash the dishes. I could see that this was hot gossip to be shared, but it would probably come out like *American women make their husbands do dishes and chores!*

This was only my first three cups of tea with them. It would take many more to bring about change in the way they think about things. Shifting a culture is about as difficult as trying to push a planet out of its orbit. But we, as volunteers, do try having some of those conversations about the role of women, about HIV/AIDS, about birth control, about life. It takes drinking at least 300 cups of tea with them to get to know someone and create that bond of trust. Every once in a while somebody totally gets it, and every once in a while a volunteer experiences that these people totally accept them for who they are, and love them, and will put their lives down for them. Thus, slowly, some of their ways rub off on us and some of ours on them, and both of us evolve. Both cultures are enriched, theirs and ours.

Once I asked Moussa why I as a woman was invited to attend men's tea parties.

"Foreign women are like men," he said, and meant it.

It is true that foreign women are treated very differently. It is as though they are sexless. They are given the privilege of being a part of the men's discussions and the men's 'superior' environment, where intellectual talk happens and decisions are made. Malian men seem to like working with foreign women. We can go anywhere alone without trouble. We are independent and not accountable to them. As such we are their colleagues.

Being a married woman with grey hair, I get away with a lot. I can afford to be humorously brazen, like the time we were talking about birth control and I asked why Malian men discouraged it.

"To have many children is a blessing from Allah, and who are we to do go against his will?" they said.

I had gotten to know the men quite a bit, and knew they enjoyed my company. I did not hesitate to tell them that Allah had given them a brain, and who are they to go against his will to use it. Jokingly, I said that I thought Malian men prefer to think with their penises. They laughed and laughed.

"Now if you were using your brains, how many children would you have?" I continued.

I am not sure that a twenty-three year old volunteer could get away with that. With me, there is no sexuality involved.

The World Bank lists Mali as one of the poorest countries in the world, ranking it 175 out of 187 on the UN's 2011 Human Development Index. Life expectancy is just 51 years, and the average gross domestic product per person is $691. For six decades, development agencies (USAID, the IMF, UN agencies, NGOs, church groups, etc.) have come with solutions in hand, guaranteed to solve all that ails this country. Each tractor, each new improved high yield seed, each maternity center and school was a lottery win for those who benefited. Some years later, after the tractors broke and they didn't have the know-how to fix them, and they couldn't afford the custom fertilizer for that super seed, and couldn't afford to staff the schools and maternities, those tractors and school buildings sit idle as monuments to somebody's good intentions or tax write-off.

Yes indeed, they are miserably poor materially, and cannot afford to fix the roof leaks of their lives. They can only mop up the puddles. If the tractor breaks, they revert to doing things by hand; a nation of copers rather than fixers. When you bring fixers and copers together, you have one beautiful codependent relationship. We feel good doing good, and they don't complain about having things done for them, and will praise Allah for their good fortune. A happy marriage – or is it?

During our pre-service training, Peace Corps had several sessions on how we should approach working in the village and facilitating change. *What is sustainable development?* was a big topic of discussion. My favorite quote from the training session was from Roland Bunch. Here is what he had to say about it:

> *Sustainable development is a process whereby people learn to take charge of their own lives and solve their own problems. Development is occurring where people are gaining the self-confidence, motivation, character traits and knowledge needed to tackle and solve the problems they have by actually tackling and solving those problems. The process whereby people learn, grow, become organized and serve each other is much more important than the greener rice fields and the fatter coin purses that result.* – From *Two Ears of Corn*, by Roland Bunch.

How do we achieve this lofty ideal? As volunteers, we live with the locals, learn their language, their ways. We learn *why* they do things the way they do, and what they would like to see changed for themselves, or for their children. We ask them what solutions *they* have for getting there. We ask what they need in order to achieve those dreams, and how we can build their capacity to get there. That is the tall order that Peace Corps volunteers try to fill; and being doers and fixers by nature, our biggest challenge is to take the time to drink those 300 cups of tea with them, before we start projects.

That's the theory. In practice there is a major clash of cultures. We and they are rough rocks in an agitated jar, banging against each other: our agenda versus theirs; our solutions versus theirs; our values versus their values.

"How is it that they don't just get it?" we ask ourselves.

They just don't get the germ theory of disease; they just don't get that mosquitoes cause malaria. Some still think that they get malaria from eating mangoes! Why is it that they just don't get that saving money is a good thing? (But then, most Americans don't get that either). They don't get the most obvious of things. Any female who has had her genitals mutilated – why would she want to inflict that on her daughter? So many issues have the simplest solutions, but they don't get it.

Many aid workers never get beyond this level of thinking. But then again, just maybe they failed to drink those three hundred cups of tea with the people they came to help, listening to their stories, their dreams and their solutions: because that is what it takes. Change comes one person at a time, and most of the time there is no glamour and no recognition. We don't even know whom we have touched, or how.

Just maybe when I am done with the Moringa training I will start a men's group, where we can discuss the role they play in determining the future of their country and of their kids, and I can sell them on family planning. I have a couple of men on my side now, just another four or five million to go!

I Prefer Men

Empower a woman, feed a family; empower a man, feed his ego is the current favorite idea in the development community. I wondered why I preferred working with men, and felt I could sway the way men thought and thus buy a better life for the women. The truth is the women's clique at the clinic gave me one big cold shoulder. Only once was I invited to have tea with them.

I was feared for my independence, for wanting to promote women. These women reminded me of my mother, too afraid to let their daughters grow up to be anything other than wives and mothers. My freedom, my self esteem, my propensity to challenge the status quo was scary. Encouraging girls to study and have dreams and ambitions was scary.

Aren't you afraid your husband will leave you? Aren't you afraid of being alone? Aren't you afraid of life? Aren't you afraid...? The old way is better.....it is secure ...and Allah sanctions it, they said. Maybe I acted too soon. Maybe I had not taken the time to drink the three hundred cups of tea with them, or maybe it was something else.

They were my mother, pushing the same fear and God buttons in me. My dearest mother was so afraid for me that she spent an inordinate amount of time praying on my behalf, begging God to take care of me, to forgive me for my foolish ideas. How she cried before I left to complete my education in England. No doubt she would miss having me around, but that is not why she was crying and fraught with worry: she was honestly concerned that if I had an English education and went to University, nobody would marry me. That is, no "good Muslim Indian family" would want me as their daughter-in-law. I would be "spoiled goods," she said.

"Do you want to be alone and lonely? Why don't you tell daddy that you don't want to go. We'll send you to secretarial school..." she cajoled.

No way was I going to tell daddy that I didn't want to go to England. I was going to finally get to climb the Tower of London and be free of parents. I was counting the days and hours to when I would board the Boeing 707 to London, all the while praying hard to that same God to ignore my mother's earnest requests.

My father was a man of the world who loved to read and dance and wine and dine. He loved the theater and music and travel. He wanted his daughter to have a good education and to have choices. He understood that the world was changing and, now that Tanzania and Kenya had got their independence from the British, that life for the Indian community was not going to be the same. While nobody knew what the future would hold, a good education was the best insurance policy he could buy me.

I did come back married to a white man, fulfilling one of my mum's worst nightmares, but in the end she thought David was a diamond. I have always credited my father for who and where I am today. The Malian women at my clinic, like my mother, were keepers of traditions. Foremost among those traditions is teaching young girls their proper place in family and society, regardless of how repressive that might be. I realize now that I lack respect for women who keep women and girls down, and thus I lack what it takes to work with them. Without even thinking about it, I chose to work with men. At least they welcome me and all my eccentricities into their world.

It is true that I did not respect my mother. I rebelled against all that she held sacred, like the unforgiving god, her subservience to men, and her need for approval from the community. Having said that, today I appreciate more than ever the role she played in making me who I am. By trying to hold me back, she made me strong and resilient; by having to fight against her religiousness and piety, she instilled in me the importance of spirituality. By her example of constantly doing good for others, I learned how fulfilling being a volunteer can be. My father gave me the opportunities, but my mum gave me the tools to make the most of the opportunities. They both live on in me, though I have yet to learn how to empower women other than by example.

Let the Training Begin

Something about being back in Bamako's fastest lane throws you into a different Universe so revved up that it wipes the memory slate clean. Was it only last week when I was sleeping in my own bed, pondering the life of Steve Jobs?

The sixty-page document that I boldly labeled *Moringa – The Implementation Guide* has been sent to the printers. Phew! What a game of snakes and ladders it was getting our ever-busy PC bosses to take initiative. Several times, I plonked myself in their offices and refused to move until they did what I needed them to do. I made the deadline, though how I wished I had another week to send the document to a variety of reviewers. It is too late! Already, it is time to greet and welcome the forty newly arrived trainee volunteers.

"Finally we are here on African soil; finally we made it into Peace Corps; finally our adventure begins." Their energy and enthusiasm was super-infectious. Just like us nine months ago, the newbies were filled with questions – wanting to absorb it all *NOW*; wanting to be old hands *NOW*. After showing them their huts, our first task was to teach Potty Training 101, how to squat down on that little hole, the gateway to hell. That slowed them down a whole bunch. I witnessed with great empathy their first moment of doubt, the oh-my-god-what-have-I-signed-up-for feeling that they tried so hard not to show. We, the trainers for this new cohort, knew that this too shall pass.

Moringa teaching materials

Nine months later, all my doubts and trepidations have morphed into *I am so lucky to be here*. How long that will last, I don't know, but I will take my highs as they come. Nine months later, we have lost 11 people from our Stage of 61. A few chose early termination; several were med-sepped (sent home for medical reasons), and one got pregnant.

I had my flip charts ready with hand-drawn pictures of carrots, glasses of milk, an egg, bananas and oranges, showing them all the nutrition that Moringa leaves contain. I remembered how I had tried to do a similar presentation in Bambara at my clinic so many months ago, reading haltingly from the manuscript about the virtues of the miracle tree. I remembered how the project began, expanding hand in hand with the sense that finally I had something to contribute. Our new trainees were very eager to start work! They couldn't even say "good morning" in Bambara yet, but they couldn't wait to become Johnny and Jenny Moringa Seed. We gave them each a small bag of seeds to take to their homestay villages, to plant at each of their family's homes. Chapter one of the Implementation Guide had began to unfold.

Thanksgiving

Who would have thunk that I would be eating pumpkin pie for breakfast on the day after Thanksgiving in Mali? Who would have thunk that I'd have all the pleasure of licking my fingers after eating a mother plateload of real butterball turkey, cornbread stuffing, gravy, mash, sweet potatoes and green beans?

I was at the training center for Thanksgiving with all the newbies who had been brought back specially from their homestays, knowing full well how near and dear this holiday is to Americans. The only way to cure homesickness is to be among other Americans in the holiday season.

The *refectoire* (our eating hall) burst into activity. Baskets of beans, sacks of onions, potatoes and sweet potatoes, bags of flour, whole pumpkins and random cans of treats that various volunteers had received in care packages from home, all of it was lined up on several of the long tables. Five of us volunteer trainers took it upon ourselves to cook for the 100 people who would attend our feast of giving thanks.

Our Malian kitchen crew had little idea about how to stuff and cook the turkeys, which had been donated by the American Ambassador and the Country Director. These butterballs were especially flown in from America. The volunteer trainees eagerly signed up as onion choppers, garlic smashers, and green beans top-and-tailers. They clustered around the refectoire tables, onion tears rolling down their faces. Our regular kitchen staff squatted on their stools peeling potatoes. I loved being the kitchen queen, pouring my creative juice here, there, and everywhere as we compared recipes and then created new ones to fit the ingredients we had. What do you do when you have just two small cans of cranberries, one real pumpkin, two bags of apples, a single bottle of marmalade and a hundred people to feed? You bake sweet potatoes with chunks of pumpkin and apple, and drizzle it with a marmalade ginger cranberry glaze! It tasted as good as it sounds.

Thanksgiving food prep

It was a first for the Malian cooking and training staff. They were used to having a day off, and thus had no clue about this most American of festivals. They dined with us by candlelight, on tables with actual table cloths, and with centerpieces featuring paper turkeys and plastic pumpkins nestling on a bed of dried leaves. The ultra-Americana decor came to us courtesy of one of the parents, who thought Thanksgiving in Mali would just not be the same without the kitsch. She was right. These were conversation pieces, forcing us to explain to our Malian guests the story of how the Indians saved the Toubabs from starvation, and in thanks we took their lands and massacred them… But we celebrate their generosity to this day.

Four weeks into their training, the bedraggled-looking newbies were settling in nicely. No one had split, though I'm sure they had had many a moment of doubt as they dashed for the *negen* (out-house), wondering if they'll make it for the umpteenth time that day. They probably questioned their sanity for signing up to live at the edge of the Sahara for two years. Hell, I still have those feelings, and I am not even in a mud hut and have a flush toilet. In fact just the other day, when some text messages warned us that various Europeans had been kidnapped, my first thought was not fear but excitement at the possibility of getting temporarily evacuated. A free trip to Morocco maybe! A few days later we got the all-clear and it all fizzled out. Just as well, because all my work on Moringa would have been for naught.

The sessions I gave on Moringa were extremely well received. David wrote a song on the virtues of Moringa set to the tune of *Waka Waka Hey Hey*, which had everyone dancing. The volunteers and their Malian counterparts were all very anxious to jump on the 'let us fight malnutrition' donkey cart. Who knows, together we may actually make a difference and reach some kind of tipping point. Wouldn't that be awesome! Even if it makes a difference to one child, it would have been worth it. Low expectations yield more surprises, and I live for those.

After spending all of November at the training center, I finally returned home to Kayes and my husband. How glorious it was to sleep in, and to rearrange furniture in preparation for the holiday season. We have been invited to go caroling with the missionaries in a pirogue on the Senegal River. Our small band of volunteers is already organizing a feast, most likely to be held at our house on Christmas Eve. There will be no Christmas pudding to flambé at the table, but I did find some chestnuts and canned asparagus at the fancy Bamako Toubab shop. It will be a very special tinsel-free, gift-free holiday season.

The Missionaries

The last thing I had expected of my Peace Corps Service was to fall into the company of missionaries. Not only that, but I actively sought them out. As respectful non-believers, we attended their bimonthly prayer meetings in English; we joined them for sing-alongs and game nights; and on December 23 we'll be with them on the river in small canoes, belting out Christmas Carols to the hippos and crocodiles, despite the often-told horror story of how the boat sank the last time they did this! And no, the crocs did not eat the missionaries all up.

Why, might you ask? I don't mean singing to the hippos and crocs; why befriend missionaries? From his grave my grandfather is also screaming *why, why, why???* In our family we were never allowed to forget Sakri, my father's sister, who was sent to the

Catholic convent school in Dar-es-salaam. This was back in the late 1930s, when teaching young Muslim girls even the three Rs was hardly fashionable. But my modern grandfather wanted his daughters to be educated, and thought they would be safe in the hands of the nuns. Were they? Sakri converted to Christianity and vanished behind the bars of the nunnery. She was only 17 or 18 when she took her vows. A few years later she contracted tuberculosis, and the nuns would not let my grandparents take her to Europe for treatment. In fact they were not allowed to see her at all until the last hours of her life. She died at 22, leaving behind a heartbroken family who couldn't even bury her using their own Muslim rites. Needless to say, their love and tolerance for Christian missionaries and Christians in general was somewhat diminished.

Where I come from, we could not tell the Catholics from the Baptists from the Lutherans from the Evangelicals. They were all Christian, white, and arrogant enough to think theirs was the only true God. It reminds me of the present-day media stereotype of

Muslims; they are all suspect; each one could morph into Osama Bin Laden and join the Islamic jihad, without notice. So it was with my family and community back then. Every Christian was suspect: very smart, but totally amoral.

I am said to be the carbon copy of Sakri, whom I never met but have been likened to all my life. It is ironic that years later, when we moved to Hawaii, I ended up attending a little Hawaiian Catholic Church for a few years. During that time I contracted and was treated for tuberculosis. Even stranger was the photograph of Sakri that sat on my dressing table – it began to fade for no obvious reason. I had come to see her as my guardian angel. As I fell away from the church and stopped going, her image all but disappeared from the black and white photo, taken on the day she took her vows, and the only memento our family has. (The picture of her is a scanned copy of the original, before it faded away).

Our missionary friends here are hardly the dour soul-saving nuns of yesteryear. They do take their work absolutely seriously, but also with a lot of humor and compassion. Jesus would be proud of all the Samaritans these folks eat with. Saving souls is why they are here, but forgiveness and compassion are important ingredients in their beliefs. Many of them have been in Africa for decades, and have raised their children here. Their love and dedication for the Malians is immense: like their very own flesh and blood, they care about the welfare and well-being of the kids, the parents, the communities. They speak the languages oh so fluently. Several of them are translating the Bible into local languages, and are making a huge effort to make people literate in their own tongues. They are as involved in development work as any Peace Corps volunteer, digging wells, helping them with building and farming techniques and much more. Unlike us volunteers, though, these folks have made a lifetime commitment to the people of Mali.

While I am not a believer in God in any traditional sense of organized religion, I do have a hunger and thirst for that which is spiritual. Traditionally the woods have been my church, the ocean my communion, and the wind, the birds, the rainbows, the earthquakes and lava flows my sermons.

Bereft of woods to walk in, and oceans to contemplate, I am sipping at the only spiritual font available to me here in Kayes – the missionaries. We go to services at their house and listen to their prayers and about their God. We feed off their spiritual energy, get inspired by their songs and stories. It feels good to be among them, and even though I cannot share their faith, it gives me energy and inspiration to be the best I can be; to give more of myself.

A Sahel Christmas

"Would you like to join us to go carol singing on the Senegal River?" our missionary friends asked.

Sure, why not? I have never sung to the hippos and crocs or got baptized in the river – there is something about that in the Bible, isn't there?

Kayes' entire expat population piled into the boat and launched the singing marathon with *I'm Dreaming of a White Christmas,* and ending with *Silent Night* sung simultaneously in English, German, French and Spanish. We were twenty in all, which included the German missionaries, the Cuban doctors, and the American volunteers and missionaries. I wonder what our punter was thinking, listening to us belt away for an hour while he shuffled the boat around in the river, managing to get us stuck on a rock and then valiantly jumping in to dislodge us. Surprise of all surprises, the mighty Senegal was just knee-deep. We didn't capsize, and alas, there was no standing ovation from the hippos. In fact, there were none to be seen; just maybe they are smarter than we think.

In Mali, Christmas is just another ho hum, humdrum day. There was not a single place in town where we could see (let alone buy) a strand of twinkling lights. No lit-up plastic reindeers or Santas bobbing in the wind. No schmalzy Christmas music oozing out of elevators (no elevators!) or department stores (none of those either). No reminders at all that 'twas the season to be jolly, falalalalala. Very few knew enough to say I sambeh sambeh – wishing you well for the festival – but then only 5% of the population is Christian, so what did I expect?

I did not expect a phone call at 8 am on Christmas morning.

"Would you like to join us for a Christmas service in Dar es Salaam?" It was one of our missionary friends.

Dar es Salaam, Tanzania, where I was born? That would be a divine miracle enough to turn me into a Bible-thumping believer.

"But that is a two day plane ride from here, and we would have to go to Bamako first!" I retorted

I had no idea there was an itsy bitsy village, ten miles away from Kayes by the same name (haven of peace). How could I not go when serendipity called?

We gathered in a dark little room with a table and shelves full of eclectic books ranging from Clinton's *Ma Vie* to a French encyclopedia. There were no choirs, musical instruments or robed priests, just a couple of dozen of us seated in rows, shouting out requests for hymns, which we sang a capella with all our breath and voice. Gusto-filled, heartfelt Hallellujahs and Aminas punctuated the service. I had no idea what I was saying Amen to, for it was all in rapid fire Bambara; but whatever it was, we were all in it together.

They must have slaughtered a flock of sheep for the feast that followed. While waiting for lunch, I strolled on the grounds. Behold, what do I see but a bunch of Moringa trees! Local folks are actually growing them. Happy Christmas to me. Thank you Jesus.

Moringa – a satisfied customer

Too quickly our African Christmas was over. There was nothing to put away, no pine needles to sweep up; just a year ahead to melt away that pipeline of fat around my waist. It is always good to start the New Year with some kind of purpose and a reason to live.

A Short Hop to Senegal

Base map courtesy Wikipedia Commons

Happy New year to me! I was chosen to take my Moringa show to Senegal to present to the All-Volunteers conference there, all expenses paid. Thrilled to bits, my stoked ego blinded me to the fact that Peace Corps would only foot the bill for bush taxis and buses; no fancy airplanes for the likes of me. I said *no problem*, too quickly. After all, we live just a short hop from the Senegal border.

Enthusiastically I set my alarm for 4:00 am to catch a private taxi to the bush-taxi-to-Senegal stand outside town, so that I would be the first on board to embark on the 400 mile trip to Theis. My missionary friends assured me that it would take about 9 hours. They do it all the time.

I hardly expected to be dropped off at a used car junk yard. A jumble of beat up old station wagons and sedans reduced to crumbling crunches of metal, minivans that had seen better days, and heaps of tires were strewn in front of the dilapidated thatch hangar. No lights, no electricity. Just a couple of worn wooden benches, some mats, *salidagas* (large plastic water kettles used to wash) and a table with a sleeping body slumped over it. No way could this be the Taxi Gare!

The taxi driver, seeing the *where have you brought me* look on my face, prodded the slumped man, who rose to life long enough to give me a chair, then randomly moved the mats and salidagas around before slumping back. **5 am** became **6 am**, which was when the first taxi to Senegal was supposed to have left. The slumped man was still slumped – no life, no cars, no light. There was just the big old moon and Scorpio winking down from the sky, a befuddled me, and a breeze with a cold sharp bite. I can now discourse knowledgeably about dawn in the Sahel, a subject I was sorely lacking in.

But wait, was that another passenger walking into the Gare? I tried to catch his eye to ask. He did not even look at me as he picked up a Salidaga and mat, and found a spot to wash and pray. The comforting chorus of Allahu Akbars from surrounding mosques echoed the dawn in as silhouettes of straw-laden donkey carts lumbered by on the road above. The sound of whips lashing the donkeys' backs made me pull the shawl tighter around my body. Just then a private taxi dropped off a dapper young fellow, and behind it, a second car full of turbaned guys with crisp floor-length kaftans and a container-load of bulging suitcases. Yesss, that was the end of my despair. We had seven out of the nine needed for the shared taxi, a station wagon built to hold five, outfitted to fit in seven by adding a bench in the hatchback part; but in Mali it is all about how many they can cram in, with the minimum set at nine.

There was something about those tight jaws of the turbaned fellows, whose loud combative voices smelled of violence. Al Qaeda operatives? My pounding heart added the soundtrack to my fears of being kidnapped. Fear and excitement fuelled fantasies of my valiant escape from capture, of how I would outwit them and how they would have to crawl on the floor and grovel for forgiveness – these were the new movies my brain ran for my entertainment.

I was distracted by the gaggle of ladies balancing basin loads of breakfast on their heads. They were offering hot beans and *mɔni* porridge. One lady filled up a bowl for the chef de la post, the man who was slumped over the desk but was now up. The taxi Gare was coming to life. **7 am** came and went. The dawn pinks softened the sky, but my day had already turned sour.

The four meanies pounded their fists, quarrelling rowdily with the Gare manager. Were they demanding where the 6 am taxi was? Were they threatening the guy? I didn't understand a word. The Gare manager was holding his own, but then, quite abruptly, walked away. The next thing I knew, a beat up old sedan materialized and the men were stuffing themselves and their baggage into the car and drove off. Bugger! Our almost-full car was back to three. How much longer did we have to wait? It was **8 am**. I added nine hours to that, which brought us up to an arrival time of 5pm. That would still be okay, but we needed six more folks

NOW. These bush taxis will not budge an inch if there is any breathing room in the car.

By then I was chums with the dapper young guy, conversing in French. Son of a local councilman and brother of the local Mayor, he lived and worked in Paris as a chauffeur. He said he loved New York (he visited his brother there once), and Jeep Cherokees. His dream was to buy one and drive it across the Sahara from Paris to the new house he was building in Bamako.

"Never again will I have to endure public taxis!" he said, and I totally got it. Three hours after stepping out the front door, I was still just two miles from home.

9.20 am. We had liftoff. Four of us were squished in the back seat, our hips fused together as we bounced up and down on a road that had been tortured beyond repair. Two hours later we arrived at Diboli, a town perched on the Malian side of the border, from where we had to take a separate taxi to cross the bridge into Senegal to the taxi stand in Kidira. That was so easy; there was no waiting involved. *What a civilized country* I thought, until I found I was number 3 out of the seven needed for the bush taxi to Kaolack, where Peace Corps Senegal has its Stage House.

Noontime. Eight hours on the road, and I had come about 80 miles.

> *I am hot, tired, bored and hungry,* I texted David.

> *How about some Phone sex, baby?* he replied.

> *You first…*

> *I'm taking off my shirt now, and baby I can tell you: I am one very hot dude.*

> *Yeah, so? Everybody in Kayes is hot all the time.*

> *You're a tough one, baby; I like 'em that way. Talk dirty to me.*

> *The toilets are filthy, you need a tetanus shot for the taxi, and the driver smells like halftime in a locker room.*

> *Baby I can just taste those glistening thighs, those waiting lips...*

> *Textus interruptus, my dear. Running out battery. Sorry.*

Well, that was good for a few minutes of entertainment!

1pm, 2pm, 3pm came and went. I was practicing Zen and the art of waiting in a large vacant sandy lot with temperatures so high that swatting a fly made you sweat profusely. People were wilting and snoozing, anything but moving. I wondered what they were thinking, these folks for whom so much of their lives was spent waiting. What movies were they playing in their brains? Were they dreaming of going to America, the promise of a hunger-free and comfort-filled life? Me, I just wanted to get to my destination. Why couldn't they have a scheduled departure time? Surely people would show up and fill the seats, instead of this wait-until-we-are-full departure schedule. Ah yes, this was the practicum of patience and endurance. I thought about what it means to be in the moment as I started counting my breaths. Just hot sand and nothingness.

Two more people materialized, causing a flurry of conversations. The ticket seller said he had one more person lined up who would be here soon; would I buy the last seat so we could get on our way? Yes! Yes! Anything to get out of here. I think he was counting on this Toubab to do just that, and I did not disappoint.

Finally at **3:45 pm**, the man arrived in all his finery, a golden waxed *boubou* gown, his shaved head glistening, his sharp features spelling out that he was a man who always got his way. I bet he was the school bully. He told me what a favor he was doing me to ensure an on time departure (for whom? I wondered), but he'll only travel with us if I sat in the back back – on the bench seat, squashed with two other people. We still had another seven hours of driving time ahead of us. In the moment I agreed, but anger within me flared. I paid for *two* tickets to get half a seat, just so you don't wrinkle your gown? I was already not thinking good thoughts about the Senegalese. Kind gentle sweet Malians would never do this. Would they?

Another 45 minutes passed. Who knew why. Tapes were playing fast and furious in my head about a showdown with the Golden Boubou. Having paid for two seats, why must I, an almost 60 year old lady, sit in the back back? The time came and I refused to move. The driver totally saw my point but angry conferences were taking place around me in Wollof. Finally I agreed to the compromise of sitting where I was as long as two others can sit next to me and my 'extra seat' was in the back back, if I wanted to put my bag there. Two lanky young lads had to scrunch their knees in the back back. No, I did not feel bad.

We had tie down and liftoff. The road was absolutely fabulous – my goodness, not a single pothole. Senegal was looking better. We were cruising at 90 kmh; all was good with the world. We dropped various passengers along the way until I was the only one left when we arrived at Koalak station, about 290 miles down the road. This was my stop, and now – at midnight – I had to find yet another taxi to take me to the Peace Corps house. My driver ordered me to stay in the car; he would take me! I did not argue, but then he disappeared, leaving me waiting. Ah yes; waiting, waiting for the moment I could shower and fall into bed.

Suddenly a stranger jumped into the driver's seat and waited silently. Do I get out, do I stay? Before I could decide, a furious argument ensued between him and my newly returned driver. *In another 30 seconds I'll be referee'ing a fist fight,* I thought, so I got out to look for another taxi. *Get in!* my driver yelled at me, still hot after he chased the stranger away. I could not see for the world of me where he was driving me. I called Jessica, my PC contact, to give landing instructions to the driver. All was indeed well, but when I arrived the driver wanted 5000 CFA instead of the customary 1000 CFA fare.

"I looked after her like my own sister," he told Jessica, who was chewing him out in Wolof.

We settled for two thousand CFA (about $4).

The PC Regional House at Kaolak was rocking and rolling. Music blared, kids were dancing on the rooftop. Sprawled across the rest of the house were the less energetic volunteers, dripping from sofas, chairs, and on the floor. I was both tired and wired. They had saved me a precious bed in the eight-to-a-room dorm, but I don't think I was going to get much sleep. How I would have loved a shower and a bite to eat.

Allah came to the rescue, not with food, but via PC transport. The bus was scheduled to arrive in Kaolak at 6:00 pm, but due to a mega traffic tie up, it had only just then rolled in at 12:45 am to take people to Thies. The next bus to Thies was at 6 am. By then

I had absolutely no grey cells firing, so I chose to keep going – maybe I'll fall asleep on the bus! Fat chance. The guy next to me, a 300 pound football player, fell into a comma on my shoulder and squashed me into a paté against the side panel. At **3.30 am** we finally arrived at Thies. Somebody had thought ahead and laid out 30 mattresses across the conference room floor, where I flopped, unwashed, no dinner, and with my shawl as a blanket. You'd think by then I would totally surrender to exhaustion and sleep. Evidently God was pulling a Job on me. It was the plague of one mosquito, whining in my ear and clamoring for my blood. Woe is me! I am never leaving Kayes again!!!

"Stories happen to those who can tell them," says Clarissa Estes.

She also said, "Aim towards the triumphant life full of adventures…"

Was that an adventure I just had? I associate adventure with thrills, with being pushed to the edge and coping. Waiting endless hours in barren lots for bush taxis is not a heart-pumping experience, but it is a story of what local folks have to go through to go anywhere. No wonder they are always late for work. Now I aim towards the triumphant delivery of my Moringa workshop, trying to squelch any thoughts about the return trip, where I will have to retrace my footsteps. Thank goodness for one of the joyful attributes of memory – we forget pain very quickly; otherwise I suppose women would never have more than one child. A shower, a change of clothes and a good nap totally renewed me.

I fell in love with Thies, an old colonial town crisscrossed by boulevards and graced by a panoply of old African walnut trees, and cascading bougainvillea. No open sewers, very little trash. What would I give to be a volunteer in this town, with its multitude of restaurants where one could actually have a glass of wine with dinner. Evidently PC Senegal is looking for curriculum developers who would be based in Thies. Is that temptation or what!

The Senegalese volunteer organizers invited me for a drink at the Catholic Mission. Stolen communion wine? The Catholic Mission was indeed a bar. I am sure at one time it did serve a different purpose, but its mission now is to keep volunteers well oiled. Evidently, a few years ago the compound had just a shack where the owner sold cigarettes, tea, sugar, and some beer. As word about the beer got around, he became the most popular shack in the vicinity; so popular, he was able to afford a freezer and then a real shop and some tables and chairs. The venture has grown into a beautiful terrace bar, with tiled floors and trees, built on the profits of selling one beer at time to PCVs. This is Development!

When things go well, there is nothing to write home about except to say the conference went well, the food was good, and I met some interesting people. On the return trip I had to wait a mere 15 minutes before the taxi filled to take us to Tambacounda, where I was going to spend the night at the Peace Corps regional house, and then catch the early morning taxi to the border. At Tamba I was more than two-thirds of the way there already. I was delighted that my travel karma had taken a turn. Then came the serpent offering me an apple, in the form of a kid who tempted me with the possibility of a bus that he insisted was ready to leave right now and was headed directly to Kayes. I totally fell for it. I really did want to get home so badly. He took me to the ticket office, where the clerk told me that the bus was on its way to the border. And since the border crossing takes a couple of hours, with a busload needing their IDs checked and stamped, he would drive me there and we would catch up with the bus. 10,000 CFAs please! I gave him my crisp new bill and we were on our way. How lucky was that?

I eagerly jumped in his car, but what the hell is going on? He tried to drop me off at the bush taxi stand. I was number three, four more to go. *I want my money back*, I screamed in French, remembering the ugly faces of the Golden Bubu and the Four Meanies. I regained my composure. I turned quiet to thank him for his troubles and explained this would not work for me and please take me back to the PC House. He did, and he did give me my crisp note back. I tipped him handsomely and we parted friends.

At 7 am the next morning I schlepped my bags, and – wonder of all wonders – the car filled. In 20 minutes we were on our way to the border, and as luck would have it, most of the folks in this shared taxi were continuing on to Kayes. This time I knew the drill, and got my passport stamped on both sides of the border. At the taxi stand for the onward final leg, we were told we were going by minivan and they were just loading up. Three men were already hoisting up hundred-weight sacks of peanuts and rice onto the poor old beast. I got to ride in front with the driver. All the male passengers jumped out to push start the vehicle; the engine fired and we were off, crawling at about 30 kph. I thought nothing of it, because this was a built-up area; but it turned out that he couldn't shift higher than third gear even on the open road! At 30 kph and with 90 km to go, you can do the math.

> *I should be home by lunch,* I texted David.

A museum piece: public transport

Forty kilometers later, we ran out of gas! *No problem,* said the driver. His kid would hitch a ride to the next place that sold fuel and hitch back. An hour later, another push start, and we went putt-putting along until – guess what – the van finished guzzling its 5-liter snack only 15 km down the road. Another hour of us sitting by the road side. David lifted my spirits with another charming string of phone-sex text messages, but that didn't change the basic math: if we only had one five liter container, and ran out of gas every 15 kilometers, and the kid had to hitch a ride to and from the next gas station, what time would we arrive in Kayes? I am glad I was awake during that algebra lesson all those decades ago, as my brain processed the input. The answer? "Very, Very Late."

The driver was extremely embarrassed. He flagged down a vehicle for me, and moments later I was riding on the back of a motorbike, no helmet, wind and dust biting my face, my hair in tangles. This was a serious Peace Corps offense, grounds to be dishonorably discharged: the dreaded Administrative Separation. Did I give a damn? No I did not. I did get home safely, and the nice man wouldn't even accept money towards gas. How I wish I could say that I will never do that trip again; but for better or worse, in April when we fly back to the States, we will be flying from Dakar. We'll be making the same trip, this time with two big suitcases.

My Ordinary Life

Routine, routine, routine! It makes me crazy to see how I spend inordinate amounts of time trying to create it, only to desperately run from its stranglehold. Routine certainly does allow me to get a lot done efficiently, but without that sense of the fresh and the new, I die a slow death.

Every novelty and experience morphs sooner or later into the brushing-and-flossing-your-teeth routine. I now think nothing of navigating the impromptu slop-filled rivulets that snake their way through the market's dirt roads. By now I've bobbed in and out of every stall in the market. The endless arrays of plastic doodads and glistening mounds of nineteenth-rate Chinese trinkets are no longer enticing.

Meeting, greeting, bargaining, blessing the vendors, and finally asking for the road while promising to greet everyone at home for them takes an hour or two or three every day. And that's just to buy a few ingredients, which then have to be washed and peeled and chopped and cooked. In the meantime, the laundry has been soaking in soapy water, waiting to be scrubbed and washed, rinsed and wrung and hung out to dry. If those aren't chores enough, the sands of the Sahara never let up trying to take over our little apartment, making sweeping and mopping at least once a day a must. I now have excellent qualifications to work as a maid. The only saving grace is the good fortune of not being born a Malian woman, who does all of the above for a family of eight to twelve as well as caring for the garden, caring for the kids, serving her husband, and trying to earn a little extra on the side – all the while with either a baby on her back or at her breast, or both.

There are days when I so badly want to be beamed up to some huge, impersonal, well-lit, well-stocked supermarket, where I can anonymously stroll down the aisle and load my cart with ready-made food to throw into the microwave, and voila! Dinner is served. None of this what-shall-I-do-with-the-eggplant-today so that it doesn't taste like what I did yesterday or the day before that. I used to love eggplant, and yes, I have devised 149 ways to cook and flavor it, but it is still eggplant and it's all that is available at the market other than cabbage right now.

There is a lack of veggies from August on, because all hands are in the fields to plant and harvest grains during the very short rainy season. Even the schools shut down, freeing the kids to help their families. During the rains the vegetable gardens lie fallow and are often under water, as many of them lie on the banks of the swollen Senegal River.

Now the rains are long gone, the weather is delightfully cool, the harvest is in (pretty miserable this past year), and the women are back to working their gardens. Soon I will be able to add beets, green beans, squash, and carrots to the list of what is available. That is what is most exciting to me right now – the prospect of green beans and carrots! Hillocks of water melons will appear soon, as will pyramids of oranges. Before long mangoes will be back, signaling the hot season.

Riverside Gardens

Such is my ordinary life in an extraordinary place, cooking, cleaning, working, and watching West Wing or TED talks on the computer, in bed, under the mosquito net. I am living a life in the Sahel, where all the families are extra large, all the women are hard working, the children are naked and all the men do nothing but drink tea.

This last year has pushed the boundaries of our lives to new edges, emotionally, physically and spiritually; and as each new experience wanes, that powerful feeling of "I survived, I made it" is invigorating and energizing. We made it through the hot season, hunger season, rainy season; we even acquired enough language to get a fair bit of work done and have a sense of accomplishment, despite all the discomforts and disadvantages. What made it all work? I discovered that the secret lies in turning misery into adventure.

Misfortunes and stumbling blocks are only devastating when you believe they will last forever. Repeating to myself, *this is temporary Asifa, you are having an adventure*, allows me to be more of an observer of all that happens to me and around me. Out of every misadventure and painful experience are lessons to be learned and stories waiting to be born.

The War

Lockdown! Stay put where you are, came the message from Peace Corps Security. We had just returned from a short vacation in Dogon, ready to take the shuttle back to Kayes, when we found ourselves marooned at the Bamako stage house. Protesters were raging in the capital, throwing rocks, burning cars and letting their displeasure be known. The news showed dark pictures of a smoke-filled intersection, and Malians attacking Tuareg families living in Bamako. We volunteers and the US embassy personnel were grounded; no vehicles were allowed to leave the PC and Embassy compounds. What is all this about?

There is a small civil war raging way up north. It is the Tuaregs versus the Malian Army. This is not a new enmity. The Tuaregs are a large minority group who live on the sands of the Sahara, under which lay reserves of precious minerals. There's no way that the powers that be will concede it to the Tuaregs, giving them the autonomy they seek. It is the same old story of 'You've got what I want and I have bigger army than you do, therefore, I own it.' In fact, I know of another well armed country that often wonders how their oil got under your sand (meaning Iraq). Amadou Toumani Touré, the Malian president, has managed to keep the Tuaregs appeased over the last eight years; but now, as ATT gets ready to step down, opportunities abound.

Many, many Tuaregs worked as mercenaries for Ghadaffi. Now Ghadaffi is dead; long live his ammunition! Out of work, the

Tuaregs, having raided Libyan arsenals, are returning home with their sophisticated guns to a situation that is intolerable. In the North, hunger season has already begun; it hardly rained up there last year, and thus they have already run out of food. There are no jobs. To make matters worse, due to a few small Al Queida-related incidents (mostly kidnappings), the Western world has declared the whole of Northern Mali as a no-go area, which has in turn strangled tourism and the local economy. All the NGOs and many private enterprises have pulled out of the area.

To draw some attention to their dire circumstances, the freshly armed Tuaregs attacked a government military post. The relatively badly equipped Malian military responded with a major attack, killing 41 insurgents (the official figure). If this show of power was meant to squelch the rebellion, it failed miserably. Instead it fanned the fires of civil war. The army is now moving north. Daily we see caravans of army trucks and personnel taking the road to Timbuktu, even as families there are escaping to neighboring Mauritania and Niger, areas that are also struggling with massive food shortages. Escape war to starve to death. Some choice!

Two days later the demonstrations in Bamako quieted down, and we were given the All Clear to return to Kayes, far away from all disturbances. Well not quite all; there was plenty of commotion when underdog Mali won its soccer match against Gabon to send our team to the semi-finals. Yiiiipppppeee! For a few hours everyone forgot about having little or no food to eat. They danced and hooted and hollered in the streets, and we joined right in, chanting Ma-li! Ma-li! Ma-li!

The joys of a soccer win aside, there is much speculation about the future of this country we have come to love. Will the unrest heat up as the elections in April draw closer? The presidency is up for grabs... or is it? Rumor has it that ATT allowed the Tuareg situation to escalate in hopes that he can remain president, using the war as an excuse to change the Constitution, which would then allow him a third term.

We do not fear for our safety. For us it is just another day in Peace Corps Mali. We are more preoccupied with how to help our own Malian community deal with hunger. It is only February, and already food is scarce. Apart from being grounded in Bamako for a couple of days, all these events and speculations belong to a different reality – certainly not ours. We are more likely to get hit by a truck than be kidnapped for ransom... but if we do get carted off, I promise I will write about it.

Happy to be back in Kayes, back home, and back to work.

Happy Birthday to Me

It is a blustery, cool, dust laden, sunless morning. Love the cool breeze on my skin – so refreshing and energizing – but hate the dust irritating my eyes, clogging up my pores, my lungs, and turning my hair into unkempt furry rasta twirls. The river and the trees are out of focus. How many years of living where the air is pure is it going to take to clean out my lungs and get rid of this cough? I'm going through oodles of chapstick and shea butter. That is Mali in March. We've already had glimpses of the hot season, days when temperatures rise over a hundred and my whole body cries tears of sweat. Every cool day is a bonus – one less hot day, and one day closer to us taking off on our six week vacation. We are so looking forward to escaping the hot season, but first I have a birthday to celebrate.

I'm still flighty, feisty and fleet-footed at fifty nine – though I might add that there was a distinct shortage of flattering f words to choose from for that alliteration. Fifty nine is a pretty high number to get my head around. Forty is how I feel, which was what my mother said about herself when she turned eighty. Okay, so she did not quite say she felt like she was forty; but she did wish we would all stop saying she was eighty.

"That's how old old-people are," she said, and to her, she was definitely not old.

I know the feeling mum, but I wonder what old is? In my eyes she was what *old* looked like. She needed bars in the bathroom, a high seat on the toilet, and bulbous handled forks and spoons to get her arthritic twiggy fingers around. At eighty her body seldom got out of first gear, but her mind? She drove me nuts with her feats of logic, coming up with the most convoluted plans to do the simplest things; but as she would point out, if I did it her way, I would save 30 cents on a package of toilet paper!

"Take the 96 bus for 3 stops and then cross the street to take the 94 bus. You will see Safeway on your right, that's where you want to get off," she would instruct me. And that was just the beginning; the instructions got more complex. When she thought I was tuning out she would end with – "You will see, it is so easy!"

She hated birthday celebrations.

"What a waste of money; besides, what did you do to earn it? Nothing, nothing! We all get older, what is there to celebrate?"

On my birthday, the most I ever got from her was a blessing-filled letter.

"May God keep you healthy; May he keep you strong in your faith to him; May he make you successful in your endeavors; and may you always be of service to others."

When I was twelve years old and at an English boarding school, blessings did not cut it. I remember saving all my pocket money just to order a cake to be delivered at school and pretend that my parents thought me special enough to do that for my birthday. Today, how I wish I could have been blessed by her.

When the big day came, I was in Bamako for my mid-service medical exam. The Stage house was virtually empty – there were maybe four or five of us staying there, which translated into clean bathrooms, clean kitchen, computer available, no blaring television, and no slugs draped over the sofas like Dali watches, surrounded by gross plates of molding, congealing day-old food. That was gift enough, but Goodfella's Mary and Mad Hatter's Keiko, both on Med hold, had other ideas, as did Kevin. Together they cooked me hot and sour soup, peach cobbler, strawberry cookies and other orgasmic edibles. I had sworn off sugar the previous week, but who am I to say no to peach cobbler, or to an orgasm for that matter?

The test results declared my poop, urine and blood samples to be worm- and amoeba-free. The dental nurse did a half-assed job of cleaning my teeth with a drill bit. The dentist took impressions of my mouth to get me a new crown. It disturbed me that he neither took X-rays, nor did he put on a temporary crown, but sent me back to Kayes with a bottle of mouthwash to keep my exposed tooth healthy. Classically scary Third World dental care – or is it American Care that is over zealous?

The Famine

Our living room floor tiles have been slowly rising up from the cement to buckle and crackle and crunch beneath our feet. Mr. Landlord does not give a flying flame. What choice is there but to follow the Malian motto, "Never fix something if you can cope with it?" So we walk around the eight square feet of crunchy tiles like it was a precious museum sculpture in the middle of our living room. Truth is, these days we just don't have time to attend to things like floor tiles trying to escape their downtrodden lives.

Why are we so busy? We are at that point in our service (half way) where our projects are coming to fruition and the demand for our help is going up as word gets around. Several villages have invited me to help them learn about and plant Moringa. At this point there is still faith and hope that this year's rains will come, and they would like to get as much planted as possible. Each wind storm has us madly scuttling to put things away and batten down the hatches, raising our hopes that the clouds it brings will dump on us. Minutes later though, the wind drops dead and the laden clouds float away. As the weeks pass, the furrows on every farmer's brow deepen.

Although it is only March, some of the farmers are already abandoning their fields of wilting seedlings. The last major drought was in the mid eighties, a few of the old ones remember. They are slaughtering their animals and moving into towns, into refugee camps across the border, and to anywhere else that may offer a chance of hope, of food. One teacher told us that twelve family members have moved into her one little room. She is the only wage earner. Drought and political instability walk hand in hand at the desert's edge, where there have already been more clashes between the Tuaregs and the Malian Army.

As volunteers, we are not relief workers and cannot give money or food to our village families; but we can help reduce disease by giving training on repairing and maintaining wells, on eating beans instead of rice (if they have a choice), and other survival skills. These hardly help those writhing with hunger pains, or the children too hungry to cry. We are desperately searching for answers by brainstorming with other volunteers and local organizations. International aid organizations are mobilizing their resources. The prediction is, the famine is going to be a bad one. Instead of distributing food, they are talking about distributing money to villages to buy food – a bit like food stamps, you can choose what you want and need. Doing what is best for the people is laced with political agendas, and greedy opportunities. Greed and hunger is a marriage made in heaven... for the profiteers.

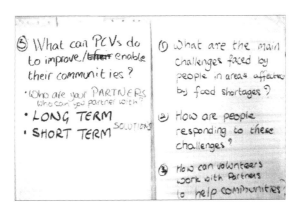

Here in Mali, emaciated bodies abound, as most families subsist and try to make it on a dollar a day. Do they see themselves as poor? They live as though there is no tomorrow, just eat and share what they have today. And tomorrow? Allah is merciful, and he will provide. When I wrote about this attitude to a friend, she shot back, "Isn't it wonderful that they live in the moment?

We have so much to learn from them." Is it really true that Malians live for the moment? Or is it that life is so painful that they can only deal with that one moment at a time, taking advantage of whatever opportunity for joy there is?

These are early days of the famine, and in the face of hopelessness I find myself praying that Allah is indeed merciful and that he will provide. Allahu Akbar! I can see the strength, courage and hope that absolute faith gives these people. Where can I buy some?

A Family Emergency

5:00 am. The phone rings. It is one of our Medical Officers. "Washington called," she says, causing my heart to race. Is it David's dad?

"Call your aunt." It is a Vancouver number she gives. Oh my dear God, something bad has happened to my family? I pace up and down to recover from the punch and gather the courage to call my great aunt.

"Asifa, it is about Zarina…. the doctors have given her less than 24 hours to live. Her kidneys are failing."

Numb, dumb and dazed, I paced frenetically, mentally willing myself to end up in London by dear Zarina's bedside. My dearest aunt, my confidante, the healer of my hurts; it is not possible. She cannot die. I was going to see her in just a couple of weeks. Please wait. Don't die. I called Zarina's home phone; her brother answered.

"Yes, it is true she is not doing well. No, there isn't any hope."

It hurt so much, I started to cry. I wanted to go to London *now*. My brain kicked in, making lists. Book flights; pack; call Peace Corps for permission and to pick up my passport; find someone to give my Moringa presentations; all this and more before catching the night bus to Bamako. The list of to-dos passed like ticker tape through my head over and over, punctuated with *Zarina is dying*. She can't. More tears. *Stop pacing!* I ordered my brain. *Buckle down and start doing*. To hell with breakfast. *I am not hungry*.

The day drowned in a frantic flurry of to-dos. At 8 pm I boarded the bus, ready to be lulled by the engine whirr into sleep. Two hours later the bus broke down beyond immediate repair. Who needs sleep? We had to wait for a replacement bus, one of the passengers explained in Bambara. I fell into despair. I didn't really believe that there was a replacement driver and bus; and if there were such a thing, it wouldn't happen in my lifetime. This is Mali! It was 10 pm and we were stranded in the middle of nowhere on the road between Kayes and Bamako. While the rest of the passengers made themselves comfortable by the roadside, settling in for the duration, I churned. The nightmare-23 hour journey to Senegal was still fresh. If that happened again, I would miss my flight. Had to have a plan B, but I couldn't think of any options. Besides, I could not call anybody; I had no bars on my phone.

"Allah is great," a fellow passenger tried to comfort me.... and just like magic, the replacement bus showed. I was the last one on, and got the only seat left, in the very back row. It turned out to be super comfy – loads of leg room, and the seat reclined as much as a business class airline seat. Well, actually it was stuck in the reclined position, but who's counting? The rest of the bus ride was a dream come true – no music and no lights. Allah is truly merciful and great. We rolled in to the capital at 8.30 am.

The Last Plane out of Bamako

Had I not churned and worried, surely the rescue bus would have not arrived and I would have been left stranded in Noplace, Mali, missing my flight, forfeiting my ticket and driven to eating worms. Dr. Dawn arranged the emergency dentist's appointment to have my crown fitted, while our volunteer coordinator personally drove me to Air France's downtown office to do an early check-in.

At noon, security warnings jammed my phone.

> *Military demonstrations in Bamako. All vehicles return to the yard; all staff go home now. All volunteers are grounded.*

"But, but but, I have an emergency dentist's appointment and I have a plane to catch..." more churning and worrying.

Dr. Dawn took me in her personal vehicle to the dentist's. Funny, it felt like just another day in the city – business as usual, with no signs of protesters or the military. Though the dentist had let his staff go home, he stuck around to fix my tooth. I was totally done within the hour, and thought nothing of hailing a taxi to take me back to the Peace Corps office. But as we were crossing the Niger, for no apparent reason everyone on the bridge began making frantic U-turns. Out of nowhere, motorbikes from the other side came at us like a blast of bullets. In the midst of this confusion, my cab driver tried also to turn his car around without getting beaned by the hurtling bikes. The army had taken the bridge, they said. I was back at the dentist's.

Three hours later, and after many conversations between Peace Corps staff, the dentist and me, it was decided that the dentist should personally drive me back to the bureau. That was the safest. The bridge had reopened, and all appeared calm. By then I had lost almost four hours of work time that I had counted on, to prepare the presentation I was supposed to give in a couple of days so a stand-in could give it. But I was in high gear. I was in the fast lane. I was super woman accomplishing great feats, powering through my checklist before I boarded that plane.

By 6.30 pm I was done enough to grab a bite to eat before my ride took me to the airport. I checked e-mail one last time. Four new messages:

Message 1 from Air France: >*We regret to inform you...* they had cancelled tonight's flight!

Message 2 from my uncle.... Zarina had just passed away.

Message 3 from the American Embassy security ... >*The army has taken over the radio. Stay put. Make sure your phones are charged.*

Message 4 from my sister in law in California .... >*Are you okay?* She had heard on BBC that there was a coup in Mali.

"No coup!" the volunteer coordinator said, when I called.

"But what about Air France?" I blubbered.

"Don't worry, he laughed, "I'm coming now to take you to the airport."

At the airport I stood amazed as he, a Malian, gave the Air France lady, also a Malian, a thorough dressing-down in English.

131

"Brussels Air has a flight leaving within the hour and AF better put her on that," he barked.

"It is not possible," said Air France; "she can apply for a refund in the normal way," she said as forcefully as she could in her faltering English.

Here I was, my fate hanging by a thread, and all I could think of was *Why are they not speaking in French?* The coordinator told me later that for a Malian to speak in English means you are powerful; otherwise she would not give him the time of day. Hell, I could have fought my own fight, if that was the case. Still I was grateful for the intervention and interpretation.

The Brussels Air lady was the heroine for the night. Knowing I was going to London for a funeral, she personally walked me through the security fast lane and out to the shuttle bus to the plane ahead of everyone else. On the runway, we waited and waited. Meanwhile my phone was ringing off the hook. It was embassy security and various Peace Corps staff.

"Where are you? Where are you? Where are you?"

"On the plane; on the plane; on the plane!"

"Are you okay?"

My battery was running low. I had no idea what the fuss was about, so I switched my phone off.

The next thing I knew, they had shut the door, hastily asked us to fasten our seatbelts, and off we went, leaving the other passengers to their own fate in the terminal.

It turned out that I was the last person allowed to board the flight. It was not until we landed in London that I learned the army had taken over the airport. Air Brussels was the last flight allowed out, before the airport shutdown indefinitely. The military had captured the presidential palace. ATT, the Malian president, had vanished. Indeed there had been a coup, but hardly anybody in Mali knew it. It was a bloodless takeover, but what was next? I would have to wait and see.

Evacuation

In these last few weeks, we've been through the wash and spin and wring cycles again and again. We are still feeling dizzy and crumpled and washed out, desperately in need of some serious hammock swinging time. A colorful drink with an umbrella lazily floating in it wouldn't hurt either.

What's going on with us? On Sunday April 8, eighteen days after I had left on Air Brussels, all Mali volunteers were evacuated to Accra, Ghana. Peace Corps Mali operations were officially suspended. The volunteers were allowed one suitcase on board the specially chartered flight. The destination? An Accra beach-front resort called "The Palms."

My fellow volunteers had been consolidated, deconsolidated and consolidated again until the order came to pack one bag and come to the training center in Bamako. Behind the scenes, Admin prepared to evacuate all 188 of them.

As for me, that fateful night at Bamako airport was the last I ever saw of Mali. In the end, I never was allowed to return from London, where I stayed for a little more than a fortnight. Instead,

Peace Corps Washington booked me on an overnight flight via Casablanca, arriving in Accra at 6 am on Easter Monday morning, just a few hours after David and the others. A SWAT team from Washington (Counselors, financial and admin advisors, doctors and nurses, career counselors, logistics virtuosos and more) was already there to meet us.

Although we could see the palm trees swaying from the conference room windows, sadly the air conditioning blocked out the music of ocean waves thundering onto the beach. From 8 am until 7 pm we jumped from counseling sessions, to sessions on how to fill out the forms that mark the end of our service, to medical tests, to updating our resumes. We struggled to keep our brain-dead bodies going to meet all the paperwork deadlines, write our descriptions of service and make uncountable decisions that would affect our lives after Friday the thirteenth, when we would be sprung back into civilian life. Should we sign up for another assignment? Should we go back to Hawaii – but if we do, where will we live? Should we take the slow road back home? Who should we bequeath all our household goods to in Kayes?

Coincidentally, our close of service date was exactly one year after we were sworn in at the Presidential Palace. Once we were signed, sealed and ready to be sent off, we had one more final session – the closing ceremonies.

Two hundred chairs were laid out theatre style, a program on each chair. Each cohort (Risky Business, Team America, the Kennedys, the Mad Hatters and the Goodfellas) sat together one last time. This was the final farewell, a heart-wrenching experience like the celebration of the life of a very beloved friend now gone. It was an untimely death that shattered all our lives.

Each of the staff told us we were the best; they consoled, encouraged and thanked us, each in their own way. Adama, our APCD, told the same story he had told me many months ago, of how his life changed because of a Peace Corps Volunteer who often came to have lunch with his family when he was a kid.

"She didn't even know how she influenced me. It was because of her that I stayed in school, paid attention to books. It is because of her I am standing here today, as assistant program director."

It turned out that the coordinator of our COS conference, Jackie, was that very same young volunteer who had come to lunch all those years ago and changed Adama's life. Tears rolled down my cheek as Adama continued,

"Do not think your work in Mali has amounted to nothing. You have touched the lives of many and don't even know it. I thank you on behalf of all your Malian families and colleagues for the love and work you have poured into my country."

The stories came from the heart. There were no theatrics, no rehearsed lines, and yet each of these stories made us laugh, they made us cry, they cradled us and they had us spellbound. They were filled with humility, gratitude and wisdom.

"In giving yourself, you find out who you are," said one.

"You cannot change the world, but please believe that you make difference," said another.

As volunteer speakers offered their thanks to the staff on all our behalf, I was sobbing as though my mother had just died. The reality of *our life in Mali is truly over* was sinking in. There would be no more twinkling-eyed little kids running across the street yelling

Toubab! Toubab! and then lighting up like Christmas trees when I shook their hands. Indeed, to our Malian friends we are now dead Toubabs, who have disappeared from their lives almost as suddenly as we parachuted in.

For us there will be life after Peace Corps Mali. The PC staff had mobilized everything within their power to ensure a smooth transition into our next lives. They moved mountains in five days, pulling all-nighters to review 200 resumes, perform our end of service medical exams, provide us with emotional and logistical support, match us up to new assignments, and so much more that we are not even aware of, all to ensure that every little nitpicky detail was taken care of. They did this with so much compassion, with love and smiles. I am truly in awe of our Peace Corps staff, and so grateful to them all. To say it was a difficult transition and an intense week is a major understatement.

In the midst of making a million life-changing decisions we said goodbye to each other, exchanging addresses and friending people on Facebook. We were doing all we could to solidify our memories, our friendships, all the while slogging through the million hours of paper work that only a government can demand. We did it. It was all over. Our Peace Corps life ended at the stroke of midnight.

The End

Weary and depleted, I fell into a poolside lounge chair and stared out into the ocean.... In two days we were to fly back 'home,' whatever and wherever that is. I felt incomplete, not at all ready to return to our old lives. We had signed up for a project in Ghana, but that would not start for at least a couple of months.

That in itself did not even begin to satisfy the need to finish what we had started in Mali – it was my Malian family I yearned for.

I know I have murmured quite a bit about moving on and away from Kayes' heat and sandstorms – they were unbearable. But I really didn't think anybody up there was listening, and this was not what I had in mind. My heartbreak came from not being able to say thank you or goodbye to Ousmane and Moussa, to my vegetable lady, my tailor and so many more; it came from having to abandon work that we had started, and which was right on the verge of taking off. Between the coup and the famine, *this* was the time when we needed to be together with our families in Kayes. I had abandoned them. It remains a scar in my soul. I had no idea how much of an attachment I had actually formed with this life on the edge of the Sahara. Another year would have been just right... But it was not meant to be.

Postscript: June 2012

It was just over a month ago that we left Accra, and yet my whole 15 month Peace Corps experience has already been filed into the Previous Lifetime archive of my mind. There are moments when, in retelling our stories and showing pictures of the friends we made, people we worked with, and the kids who just jumped in front of a camera, that the chorus of *Toubabu*, the bean and donkey-eating jokes and all the rest of it floods my head, putting lumps of longing in my throat. How I miss Mali in those moments of remembering. I still feel sad that I was not able to say goodbye and show my gratitude, that I was not able to finish what I started. David feels the same way. I still feel remorse at abandoning my Malian family at the time of their greatest need, though the guilt is passing.

For the brief time we were back, life in America swallowed us up. Our family and friends fed and fêted us, swaddled us with hugs and tears of joy. What joy it was to drink water straight from the tap, or simply throw our dirty clothes into a machine, or just to speak English and have everyone understand. It would have been so easy to slip back into life as we knew it. But the African magnet was still pulling us to return and continue with our service, our adventure. My fear is that the longer we stay away, the weaker our heart's desires will get. We have very flaky hearts! So we wait for Peace Corps Ghana to summon us. They assure us it will happen. "Think glacier," the Director of Training said the last time we spoke to her. We just have to have faith that the glacier doesn't melt before it moves forward.

After a few weeks in Hawaii, California and Chicago I returned to London, alone. David chose to stay on in Hawaii for a couple of weeks. I am relishing being alone, being anonymous and having sod all to do other than sleep, eat, and take long walks. I am experiencing serious systems failure. For the last week, I could not boot up enough to even check my e-mail, or read, or do anything but watch movies on the telly. Slowly I am being reborn.

"After all you have gone through, was it worthwhile?" friends would ask.

I would do it again in a heartbeat. The best way I can describe my experience is to point to a popular Peace Corps cartoon of a glass half filled with water. Is it half empty, as the pessimists would say; or is it half full, as the optimists insist. What do returned PC volunteers say? "Hey – I can take a bath in that!"

That was our Peace Corps experience – finding opportunities where there were none, finding joy in the smallest things, like iced water; and finding that all we needed was a bed, a bucket, a blanket, four hooks on the wall and a hole in the ground outside, to call the place home.

That was not all. We experienced what it was to be in a community, where sharing and caring for each other took precedence over everything else. Most exhilarating of all was the sense of coming alive, being wide awake, a feeling that comes from living a new life, doing something worthwhile and being able to throw your whole self into it. Just playing and giggling with my African family as we planted trees, sipped sweet tea and exchanged stories was fulfillment enough.

Mother Theresa I am not, and that halo my American friends saw was really a tiara. Looking for adventure is something I have done since I was seven, when I ran away from home for the first time.

I had got it into my head that I was going to fight crocodiles and slay black mambas. Back then, there were no backpacks, no cell phones, just big suitcases with no wheels. In one I threw all my clothes, and my favorite rag doll with her little blue dress and bonnet, Betsy Lee; I took some bread, and the brand new jar of strawberry jam that my mother had found – a rare treat in Dar-es-salaam back then. I armed myself with my dad's machete and a hammer, and proceeded to drag this oversized bag across the wooden floor, bumpity bump down the steps and down the lane to the big road. I was out of bounds already. I got as far as the median strip on the main road – a good place to rest and lick some jam straight out of the bottle. Yummieee! The big cumbersome suitcase, that was silly, I thought, so I left it right there on the median strip and took just the bottle of jam and Betsy. As I began to cross the two lanes of traffic, who should pull up......? Yes, my mother.

The spanking that followed was not exactly filled with mercy. The thing was, she was not mad about me crossing that four lane main road, where I could have been smooshed by the Jeeps that flew down the road. She was not mad about the ruts I left in the parquet floor as I dragged the suitcase. Why did she spank me? You got it, for stealing the bottle of strawberry jam. How can you have an adventure without strawberry jam?

All my life I have taken every opportunity I could to travel and cross that median strip to the unexplored side. Most recently it brought us to Hawaii, where I established myself as a Henna artist, among other pursuits. Ten years later, being happily comfortable was not enough, and dissatisfaction set in. I found myself trapped by the crocodiles and black mambas of my brain – I am too old; those aching knees and hips, where can I take them but to bed; do I really want to be squashed by the unwashed on a crowded third-world bus? Been there and done that. Why am I always so restless and dissatisfied? I wanted to run away more than ever, to see what was on the other side and to walk into the wild with just my doll, and a bottle of jam.

A quote by Howard Thurman jolted me:

"Don't ask yourself what the world needs. Ask yourself what makes you come alive and DO THAT. Because the world needs people who have come alive."

That is it! I want to come alive, and nothing makes me come alive more than being thrown into a job where I don't know anybody, don't speak the language, and the challenge is to make my life work within that community. Before my fears could immobilize me, we joined the Peace Corps and put the house up for sale. Fortunately, my husband was on the same page.

Sixteen months later, I live to tell you that those were some of the most fulfilling and exciting months of our lives. We jumped off the cliff, and we did learn to fly. It was amazing the number of people who appeared out of nowhere to help us do just that. I am so ready to jump off the next cliff. I have faith that I will grow wings again and soar. After all, as Hilary Cooper said, *Life is not measured by the number of breaths we take, but by the moments that take our breath away.* We are looking for more moments that take our breath away, this time in Ghana.

The Toughest Job You'll Ever Love

Letters from Mali, 2011 -2012

David Drury

April 2011

Graduation Day

My name is Dauda these days, like the shepherd boy who killed a giant in the Koran. There's a fine khaki dust between my toes, and beyond the huts and hangars it's khaki and scrub as far as the eye can see, right down to the big lazy Niger River. All is quiet on this Sunday afternoon here at Tubaniso, the Peace Corps training center outside Bamako. For the first time in I don't know how long, we have two days off – yes, two in a row! It's a balmy 105 degrees / 40° Celsius, and I'm sitting under a thatched overhang (which they charmingly call a hangar), typing quietly while some of the others sleep in the passing breeze. I doused my fading New Orleans T-shirt in water from the pump a while ago, but it is dry as a bone again after lending this tired old body a sweet 20 minutes of relief.

It's only a couple days now until we swear in as volunteers, and all the heavy lifting is over. It's hard to believe that less than three months ago (on my 60th birthday, in fact) we were in Washington DC, sitting jet-lagged and drowsy in some conference room as the Peace Corps Director himself welcomed us into the service. I've got to say, it's been a fire hose of new experience. On Tuesday we take the oath at Mali's Presidential Palace, with the Prez himself in attendance. No, it's not because we are so mind-bogglingly awesome, it's because of the Peace Corps 50th anniversary celebrations. Even so: What a kick!

Drowsy days are a good time to lean back and take stock. "All right, friends and neighbors" I say to my brain cells, "How did a nice boy like me wind up in a place like this anyway?"

Nah, too much work, my brain replies. Better just to let the bits and pieces and images drift by of their own accord... Like the old New Yorker cartoon that went into my 'How come you want to do this?' essay for the Peace Corps application 19 months ago. It was a scoreboard for the baseball game between the Idealists and the Realists.

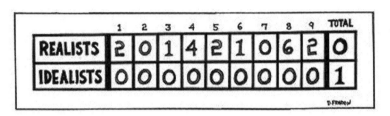

	1	2	3	4	5	6	7	8	9	TOTAL
REALISTS	2	0	1	4	2	1	0	6	2	0
IDEALISTS	0	0	0	0	0	0	0	0	0	1

Let's face it, I said to Peace Corps, there's always going to be oppression, corruption, self-interest and mindless resistance to change in this world; score a few for the Realists. But in the midst of all that are folks who patiently try to build, educate, and make things right. Just because. The builders have always been there, and they are essential to the way the world works – just as the act of doing constructive work is essential for the people who do it. When all is said and done, what have you got? Realists zero, Idealists 1.

I can't really say I'm altruistic, the essay said, but I've learned that it's WAY more fun to be a do-gooder than a do-badder. I have always been passionately curious about this world, and wherever I am assigned, it will be another piece of that magnificent puzzle. Bring it on.

They bought it, and Peace Corps advanced us to the next stage. But not before running us through a gauntlet of other questions to make sure we wouldn't strike our tents and scamper when the going got interesting. For Asifa and me, many of the questions had to do with being married and old:

"How does your spouse's reaction to stress affect your relationship?"

DD: Asifa goes for long walks in Nature. I like to kill small helpless things, like weeds and snails. We're both pretty sensitive about not taking stress out on the other person.

"We have found over the years that seniors sometimes find it difficult to learn new languages as fast as the young volunteers. How would you deal with it if you found yourself in language class struggling to keep up?

DD: I'm a very 'attaboy/ attagirl' kind of guy, and love to help people develop themselves. I'll do my best, and find other ways to get back at the young'uns for being so damn smart.

OK so that's not exactly how it went, but close enough. Some weeks later we got a call saying we were 'nominated' ... to teach English in Eastern Europe! The one and only request we had both made on our applications was to be posted to someplace *warm*. Cruel fate! It was like a story my Dad might have told, about life in the army. The recruiter reassured us that half the time volunteers wind up in a post completely different from the one they were nominated for. And lo, it came to pass.... What's that old saw about when the gods wish to punish us they answer our prayers?

As for the medical stuff: Peace Corps welcomes older volunteers with open arms, but when the nearest competent medical care is 350 miles away over laughable dirt roads, you've got to be healthy. Suffice it to say that we got ourselves injected, inspected, detected, infected, and seeeeee-lected, as Arlo Guthrie would say. We were over the crucial medical hurdle. We packed our bags in August 2010, and didn't unpack them again in a place that was truly ours for the next three and a half years.

From Hawaii, the D&A Farewell Tour jumped to the mainland to hang out with old friends and family. Peace Corps seems to evoke wonderfully warm and fuzzy images in peoples' minds (Mother Teresa meets Wild Kingdom?), and as volunteers-in-waiting we were bathed in great goodwill wherever we went. I was deeply grateful to be on the receiving end, and wanted to say "Hey, it's just me; I don't deserve this." But I didn't; I just soaked it up and remembered.

In November we got our marching orders. One final phone interview, where the recruiter asked oh-so-casually "How's your French?" and we whispered to each other "West Africa!"

Homestay – The Simple Life

Now that we're back in the training camp at Tubaniso, I have developed a case of instant nostalgia for the simple daily round of our little village. At this point, two days before graduation, it's the place where we have lived for most of our time in Mali. Mind you, Peace Corps didn't always do homestays; in the early days, most of its pre-service training took place in centralized places like Tubaniso, with limited forays outside to get a taste of real village life. Today it's completely the reverse; the village is your home during boot camp, and the training center is where you are sent, two or three days at a time, for lectures on health, security issues, community development tactics and such. -Not to mention, if you play your cards right, an occasional trip into town for lunch and a cold beer. Chronic beerlessness is a serious problem in the village, leading to weight loss and a disturbing clarity of mind. I do what I can to keep it in check.

The 60 or so newbies in our cohort were sorted out by language and scattered across a dozen villages, all in the same region. As future Bambara speakers, our little band of six was assigned to Baguineda Village in the heart of Bambara country, about 60 miles from the capital.

Baguineda welcomes you long before you get there. Turning off the last paved road, the dirt track is flanked by a mile-long honor guard of proud mango trees posted there to feed and shelter and cool the traveler. I have walked that road many times now, and it never fails to gladden the heart. Then you come upon the village itself, a dusty collection of *concessions* or compounds built from mud brick and stucco, each with its own low-slung house or two, sheds, stables, goats, chickens, donkeys, handsome guinea fowl and handsomer children. Down here there are more children than trees, it seems; it's hard for a tree to make it past childhood, what with so little rain and so many grazers with empty stomachs. The land is flat as a pool table, punctured here and there by outcrops of stark bare rock. It's an old land, and everything built upon it is the color of dirt.

On the edge of Baguineda Village

My digs were in the compound of Bakary Coulibaly, a lean, compact man in his middle forties, hair shaved down to the nub and limbs like ironwood from years of farming. A tough customer? Not at all. As is true for many Malian men, his eyes were calm and mild and prone to twinkling, and he greeted his grey-haired guest from Ameriki with sincerity and respect. "You have left home, but you have come home." And as I gradually discovered over the next weeks, Bakary was one of those quiet local movers and shakers who could always be counted on to take the first step, whether it was for better sanitation, new technologies, girls' education... I longed to tell him about the baseball game between the Realists and the Idealists, but he'd think I was crazy. *This is what the Bambara call a 'serious man,'* I thought. *A Malian mensch.*

My host family

On the Way to School

Village life in Mali is a lot like camping, only less sophisticated. At 3:47 a.m. the 936 dogs of the village (who all look exactly alike) hold an extended conversation about world politics, interrupting and shouting each other down just like the folks on Fox news. At 4:15 the donkeys chime in from the corral next door to lament their barren and unfulfilled lives. I am reminded of the French existentialists. Truly: Mali has the saddest donkeys in the world. At 5:30 it's the Muslim call to prayer; God is Great wafts across the sleeping village as the first hint of light shows on the horizon. Once again my eyelids flutter open, and I watch the tired old moon slouch back to bed. Moon, you say? Yes; the hot season is upon us, and Malian huts are like brick ovens at night. But I am cool and fresh in my REI Bug Tent, sleeping outside under the stars in the Coulibalys' walled courtyard. Asifa sleeps in her own family's compound a couple hundred meters away. Suddenly it's 6:30 and time to get up, take my morning bucket bath in the outdoor bathroom, prop my tiny pocket mirror against a fence-post to shave, and start the day.

After a hearty breakfast of mystery gruel and Nescafé, it's time to carry my girlfriend's books to school. Couples don't live together during homestay; Peace Corps knows all too well that the temptation to slip back into English is too strong. I saunter over to Asifa's compound, greeting all and sundry in the elaborate Malian way and hoping that Grampa will not make an appearance. He's a lovable old guy, lean and grizzled and ever-so-slightly dotty. Trouble is, when he gets up a full head of steam he will bless you from cap to sandals, fore and aft, larboard to starboard, take a deep breath and plunge back in again. *May peace fill your day. May God make today better than yesterday. May God return you to yourself. May the village be lighted in peace…..* I could go on like this for quite a while. A veritable Gatling gun of good will, the old man spews it out with the practiced tongue of an auctioneer. They are lovely sentiments, really, but class awaits and there is nowhere to hide. We can't even tune out and let it wash over us, since a fervent *Amina!* (Amen) is expected after each and every installment. The best we can do is mutter *Allah ka dugow mine* (May God hear all our blessings) – the traditional formula for indicating Enough already! – and back away slowly.

Our class is on the other side of the village, and along the way we pass neighbors going about their business and kids on the way to their own schools. Bambara is a marvelous language for salutes and encouragements of all kinds, not just greetings and blessings, and it's great fun to throw some cheer at targets of opportunity as we walk along. First a laborer comes past, straining against a wooden cart loaded with half a ton of firewood. *I ni baara!* I say with a nod of the head, and he breaks out in a smile. Minutes later we are enveloped by a troupe of schoolkids scuttling by in blue shorts or frocks. *Aw ni kalan!* I say, and they giggle.

Literally what I have said is "You and work," "You and study," but there really is no translation in English. It's an expression of praise and appreciation; you can use it in all kinds of situations, and they do. As I came home one day, dehydrated, bedraggled, and thoroughly out of sorts with the world, Bakary met me at the gate with a cheerfully wry *I ni sɛgɛnnen!* "You and tired" doesn't sound like much, but in Bambara it spoke volumes. If it is true that language reflects a people's deepest values – in the sense that we make it easy to say the things we most want to say – is it surprising that everyday life is so harmonious here? And what does it say about our civilization? English is a great language for put-downs, but blessings embarrass us. I wonder what we can do to change that.

Class Act

There is no schoolroom in our school. It's just a quiet courtyard with some rickety butt-floss (ahem; woven string) chairs, and two ancient blackboards leaned against some fine old shade trees. As the shade drifts hour by hour across the courtyard we move too, shifting our chairs and lugging the blackboards from tree to shining tree. Peace Corps Mali is serious about its language training, and they have assigned two Language and Cultural Facilitators for the six of us trainees. The junior LCF is a petite, personable rookie who wanted this job soooo badly, and is terrified that she will not measure up. She is Christian, which is unusual for Mali. She tries very hard, but seems more comfortable in French than in Bambara. In her stiffness I see the scars of a convent school education.

Blackboards without borders

Ibrahim Coulibaly, on the other hand, is the consummate Peace Corps veteran instructor. His grasp of Bambara goes beyond mere fluency, to where he can step outside his mother tongue and explain its arcane structures even to visitors from another planet, linguistically speaking. That's us. He takes on the task with some of the dry humor that has earned him a reputation as one of the sharpest blades in the competitive buffoonery of Mali's Joking Cousins tradition.[2] He knows the folkloric Achilles heels of every clan, and slays his opponents with the merest flick of the wrist. I've seen him do it.

---

[2] All Malians come into the world fully equipped with a set of prescribed joking cousins. These are people whom you will tease, and be teased by, for as long as you both shall live. Who you joke with is usually based on the person's family name, though it sometimes includes entire ethnic groups. You are allowed to say unbelievably rude things to a joking cousin, as long as you stay within the bounds of tradition. It's great fun, and not taken seriously.

Here is Ibrahim in action against the Coulibaly clan's joking arch-nemesis in western Mali, the Keita. Keitas are thought to be brave, but lazy. So...

Keita: *Don't you get tired of eating donkey?*

Ibrahim: *Those who never ate meat as a child sometimes confuse donkey and lamb. I have seen your father's farm.* [Shakes his head sadly]*.... So much rain, so few crops.*

Bingo! Makes me proud to be a Coulibaly. Even if it's a game, it's worth playing well, and Ibrahim brings that same sense of subtlety to his teaching. Like Bakary, he is a 'serious man.'

At noon we break off and saunter back to our compounds for lunch and a snooze – or in my case lunch, Bucket Bath Two, and some light reading or more studying. Lunch is served by daughters of the house on the woven plastic floor mat of my little room out back of the courtyard. Rice or couscous and a sauce of slick green okra or peanut, sometimes enlivened with a bit of meat or river fish. For a special treat there is the exotic Western delicacy of spaghetti with La Vache Qui Rit, a cheese-like substance concocted, far as I can tell, entirely from petroleum byproducts. I wash it all down with a cup of tepid water fetched by the kids from a tube well a quarter mile away, double-filtered and chlorinated in my Peace Corps water gizmo.

After lunch Bakary's children sometimes join me as I sit in the sparse shade of a young acacia tree with my lesson book or Kindle. The Malian government schools finally switched from French to Bambara and other local languages a few years before, and all but the youngest are way ahead of me in the literacy department. They dutifully correct my many mistakes, perhaps wondering how this nice old man could possibly get by in the world with the vocabulary of a four-year old. But the Kindle! Ah, that is pure magic. *You say there are a hundred books in that little black thing? I don't believe it.* Here, I'll show you.

Back at class in the late afternoon, we shift the blackboards and start in again. "What will everybody ask you when you come back from a trip?" Ibrahim asks. I know that one.

"*Ne sama bɛ min!*" I pipe up. "Where is my trip-gift?"

"That's a rude thing to ask, isn't it?" says Ibrahim.

"No, it's normal, even if they don't really expect to get anything."

"And if you don't have a present for them?"

"You never tell them that. You say *I sama bɛ kɔ!* I left it behind."

After class it's back to the old homestead for dinner. Bidding my host family a peaceful night, I hit the books again, by kerosene lamp or flashlight. Sounds terribly romantic, doesn't it? How I wish! Most nights it's a choice between sitting on the floor of my hut in a sweltering soup of kerosene fumes, or escaping outside to face legions of nameless bugs who show great curiosity about my homework, my eyeglasses, and anywhere that seems like a promising place to crawl in and sleep. It's impossible to reason with them.

Sometimes, though, after sunset we stay on for a communal dinner and a lecture session on Malian history and customs—

women's and men's roles, weddings and funerals, the ancient empires and the French, folktales, the roots of joking cousins. Ibrahim is a splendid storyteller, and I can still see his lively face and hands in the candlelight as he draws out some old tale.

Two brothers were on a long and very hard journey. Why, I don't know; maybe their village was attacked, and they escaped with nothing but their lives. As the days wore on, the younger brother grew more and more weak from hunger; finally he could go no farther, and just lay down in the path. The elder was stronger, and knew that the younger would soon die if nothing could be found to sustain him. Giving some excuse, he walked out far into the bush. There he took out his knife, put a soft green stick between his teeth, and cut off a large piece of his own right thigh.

"Look, I killed a baboon!" the older brother said as he limped back in to camp. "The jackals got the rest, but I rescued some for you." He cooked the meat and fed it to his brother, who soon came back to health and strength. The journey continued. At first the young one suspected nothing, but slowly-slowly the wound began to fester. Clouds of black flies followed the elder as he struggled down the path. "You are hurt," said the younger. "Let me see your leg." Then it all became clear. "You did this for me?"

Then and there the young brother made a promise to honor this sacrifice. Not only that he himself would die for the elder if need be, but that his children and his children's children's children would live at peace with his brother's family in love and devotion. So you see, peace does not come without sacrifice.

By ten o'clock I am ready for a dose of sweet oblivion, which comes on fast and lasts until precisely 3:47 a.m., when the 936 dogs of the village (who all look exactly alike) begin again their extended conversation about the state of the world...

The morning commute

Day of Reckoning

I am truly astounded at the acreage of utterly foreign words and idioms, grammar and spelling that has been crammed into this little brain over the past ten weeks. But am I now ready to sally forth into the wide world? Not really. I have managed to put down some shallow roots in sandy soil, that's all. But hell, this is not a day for hand-wringing. I passed the test! And so did Asifa.

A couple days ago we all took our final language exams in Bambara, Fulani, Dogon, or whatever local language we'll be using at work sites in different parts of the country. It was the last big hurdle of pre-service training. Since these languages are rarely written except in classrooms (and 70% of the people are illiterate anyway), your exam is just (!) a half-hour conversation with a very well-trained native examiner who was not your teacher. If you fail, and fail badly, they might not even let you swear in as a full volunteer.

The test is a peculiar experience, nerve-wracking and common-place at the same time. You meet in a little round hut, heart pounding, ducking down to get through the thatched doorway. When your eyes adjust to the darkness inside, you make out two woven chairs and a smiling Malian man who shakes your hand and asks you, in Bambara, to take a seat. A tape recorder hums away in the background. You begin with the long series of greetings that are *de rigeur* for any social contact here, and then you chat.

"How did the trip to your work site go?"

"Do you have brothers and sisters? Tell me about your family in Ameriki."

"I have never been to Baguineda village. What was it like to live there?"

Though it all seems very friendly and casual, you can see that the examiner is listening very carefully to your grammar, your vocabulary, how you frame sentences, and what you feel comfortable talking about, to get a sense of how far you have come.

Then come the more interesting questions: How come you joined the Peace Corps? What do you like to do for fun? All this is in Bambara, mind you. And if you are one of the few who did really, really well on the first part, they pull out a yellow card with questions at a whole different level, to see if you qualify for an Advanced or Superior rating. Things like "What do you think about Mali's new administrative decentralization program?" Well, duh, gee....

We didn't get yellow cards. We got blue cards (Intermediate), with topics like "You have just come to your work site and are meeting with the Mayor. Tell him about who you are, and the goals of your project, and ask some intelligent questions about the district to build up rapport." OK...... And you take a deep breath and plunge in. In the end Asifa and I both passed at Intermediate Mid, equivalent to about a year of college courses. Our language instructor told us later that we were the first two Old People to have passed Bambara at that level in years. Whew! Not that we are linguistic hotshots by any means; not a few of the young whippersnappers partied hearty while we slaved away in the days before the exam, and then sat down and chattered away with ease and grace in these totally weird new languages. Don't you just hate people like that? Actually we don't; we're very proud of them. And in any case the real language learning starts at our work sites, where people speak like regular people and aren't paid to be patient with you. We'll keep you posted.

But boy, talk about second-semester Senioritis! Les Kids (and we) are, like, SO DONE with pre-service training. Those fresh-faced lads and lasses of Week 1, poised on the edges of their chairs, notebooks in hand ten minutes before the session starts – all gone. Slowly but surely we have shifted to Mali Time. Well, we're supposed to culturally integrate, aren't we? These last languid days have also seen our medical officer, poor Dr. Dawn, making desperate efforts to instill the Fear of the Lord in her little flock in the alcohol and safe sex department. You got questions about condoms for oral sex? No, don't come to Uncle Dauda; I wasn't listening too hard. But Dr. Dawn'll set you straight, with dire prognostications about all the mind-bogglingly horrible things that will happen if you don't shape up and fly right.

April 2011

Politics

Mali lives in a very rowdy neighborhood, and it's been quite an exciting month around here politically. Riots in Burkina and Senegal, near civil war in Cote d'Ivoire, kidnappings in Niger, bomb threats against American targets in Bamako... Everybody was under restricted travel orders for a few days, but life goes on. Some of the unrest is fallout from the US/ French bombing of Libya and the fight to overthrow Mr. Gadhafi; the 'Arab Spring' revolutions that have erupted across North Africa have shaken things up in this region more than most Americans realize. It's certainly affecting Mali. Libya and Mali have been pretty chummy in recent years, with the Libyan government sponsoring lots of little aid projects in the name of Pan-Africanism. All gone now, and that upsets some people. More ominously, Malian Touregs, a Berber people from the desert North, are fighting on Gadhafi's side of the Libyan civil war. If he loses, where will they point their guns next?

Closer to home, the French have ordered their 70-odd Mali volunteers to pack up and leave. This makes us nervous, as our own situation is not much different from theirs. In fact the Peace Corps operation in next-door Niger was totally shut down just a couple months ago, after a spate of kidnappings where some French workers (mining contractors or something, not volunteers) got killed. "Oh no," we said, "you're not going to pull us out now, are you? We just got here!"

But the Country Director reassured us that, barring some radical change in the situation, Peace Corps Mali is staying put. We have had an unbroken presence in Mali for 40 years, he said, even through the bloody riots of 1991 that ended the 22-year dictatorship of Moussa Traoré and began the transition to today's democratic rule. More importantly, the Malians really *want* us here. I think that's true. Just in case, though, we have been given useful phrases in Bambara and French along the lines of –

> *I don't get involved in politics. I'm just here to help people with [health/business/ environment... fill in the blank].*

Too bad; I would dearly love to sit down with some local guys and talk politics. Still, I understand Peace Corps' concern. In this volatile climate, an argument with the wrong person could land you in big trouble.

As for Mali's other neighbors... the situation that has actually caused the most hardship here is the months-long Battle of the Presidents in nearby Cote d'Ivoire.[3] Mali is landlocked, and a whole lot of important stuff – cooking gas, for instance – comes through Ivorian ports. Not to mention the refugees: at the height of the crisis tens of thousands of Malians living in Cote d'Ivoire

---

[3] In late 2010 the sitting president Laurent Gbagbo and opposition leader Alassane Ouattara both claimed victory in Ivory Coast's presidential elections. The international community supported Ouattara's claim. Negotiations broke down as Gbagbo attacked his opponents, and a mini- civil war followed. Just a few days before this letter was written, Gbagbo was arrested with the help of UN and French forces.

fled home to get out of harm's way. It's no wonder that Mali tries to play the role of peacemaker in the region; when her neighbors go nuts, Mali gets slammed. At this point we are hoping that, with the UN capture of former president Gbagbo, things will settle down and we can fire up the kitchen stove with confidence.

The Peace Corps staff have a sense of perspective that comes from years of experience, and nobody sweats the small stuff. On the other hand, they are not fools. PC has developed a four-stage alert system (with coded messages for volunteers to be broadcast over the radio if needed... how cool is that?), not to mention triple-backup contact arrangements and detailed evacuation plans for each volunteer in case the manure ever does hit the fan. While we have travel restrictions – we can't visit Timbuktu, or even go very far north from our new home in Kayes – if worse ever does come to worst, we'll be across the border in Senegal or some-place before you can say Jack Straw. For Mali's sake, pray that that never has to happen.

April 2011

Heading Out

After swear-in I thought we would have a couple days to hang out and, you know, bask in our glory. Only in my dreams! At 6:30 the next morning we were summarily shoved out of the nest and put on the Peace Corps shuttle to Kayes (rhymes with pie), a provincial town in the far west of Mali. This is to be our home for the next two years. The Land Cruiser was stuffed to the gills with equipment, but I claimed a place in the back-back and nestled in comfortably among the water filters and duffel bags to watch the miles slide by out the rear window. "There's nothing like somebody else's baggage to smooth out the ride and give a man a cozy sense of proprietorship," I said to no one in particular. "You got that right, son" said the ghost of Mark Twain, now lounging dreamily at my side. "In my youth I was three weeks on the stage from St. Joseph Missouri to Carson City Nevada. Never would have made it but for the twenty-seven hundred pounds of the US mail she carried. We packed the coach with it from end to end, and that lazy bed was infinitely preferable to any seat designed by the hand of man." That's still true, Mr. Clemens.

It's 360 miles and 12 hours from Bamako to Kayes, plenty of time to take stock of one's place in the universe and ponder the challenges that surely lie ahead. Did I do that? Well, no; I thought about what it was like to wear a dress. Ever done that, guys? I hadn't either, until I was roped into respectability. For weddings, funerals and all ceremonial occasions your proper, dignified, 60 year-old West African male (such as myself) wears the *boubou*, a long flowing robe with wide sleeves. Mine was a magnificent blue specimen, cut from the polished cotton *bazan* fabric, with subtle patterns etched into its surface. Yes, there are pants underneath it – big, baggy things that taper down at the ankles and tie up at the waist with string – but you could be buck naked under that floor-length gown and nobody but Allah would notice.

They say the boubou comes from the Arabs and goes back to the 13th century. I wouldn't know; but I do know that wearing such a thing changes completely the way you move and comport yourself. Walking is more like wading, your stride slower, shorter, more deliberate. Crossing your legs? Forget it, unless you do it like the French or like a female. (Ouch!) Best not to attempt it. And as for going to the bathroom...

But then I'm thinking, all this recital of inconveniences misses the point. Of course it feels weird. The real question is, how do you

Sartorial splendour

ACT in a boubou? Are you somehow more feminine? Not at all, although I must say it makes me appreciate why women take so long to get out of the loo at theater intermissions; and it would admittedly be tougher to start a punch-up dressed in a full-length gown. No, the boubou's effect on normal male behavior is akin to what the sonnet does for poetry: it restricts. And in restricting, it prompts you to be just that much more formal, just that much more self-aware and dignified. Hey, what a concept! I get it. And besides – did we ever look splendid at the Presidential Palace!

May 2011

Welcome to Kayes

Some folks dream of fame and fortune; we dream of clean horizontal surfaces. Do they exist in Mali? We hope to build some shelves and find out.

For the last couple weeks we've been holing up in the Peace Corps regional Stage house, where volunteers from the villages 100 miles around come to stay while doing their banking and picking up supplies. It's a comfy old place that feels for all the world like a 1974 hippie pad, complete with a fridge, air conditioning in one room, and Internet, at least when the electricity is working. That's downright gracious living by Malian standards. But the staff did finally find an apartment for us, and it looks like we'll be moving in over the weekend. Haven't seen it yet, though; Peace Corps housing is usually handled like an arranged marriage. You don't get to meet the bride until it's too late to say no. Still, it will be a pleasant change to have someplace other than the floor to put our gear.

Our new home town is a dusty, hardscrabble little city out near the borders of Senegal and Mauritania. Kayes' one distinction is that it is reputedly the hottest continuously-inhabited town in Africa. Great for the tourism trade, eh? There's still about six more weeks of hot season to go before the real rains come, to which all Malians would add *Ni Allah sonna*, God willing. We're on the edge of the Sahel here, with desert beyond, and the rains never are a sure thing. The local folks say it'll get to 120 degrees Fahrenheit (50° Celsius) before then.

...But where are the *nice* neighborhoods?

Kayes' original reason for being is that it stands halfway between Dakar (Senegal) and Bamako; transport has always been the city's lifeblood. The town is a giant truck stop, with big-rigs lining the main road on both sides, their crews lounging outside thatched restaurants or snoozing in the diesel-scented shade between the axels, waiting for the cool of evening to start the next 12-hour leg east or west. It's a town of open sewers and plastic trash that blows, and churns, and finally decays into.... smaller plastic trash. Walking around on my first day, I remember thinking "OK, but where are the *nice* neighborhoods?"

As with so many other things in Mali, the saving grace of the place is the people.

Great Monuments of Kayes: The Unknown Politician

The Lingo and the Radio

After three weeks of going to work I still feel a little like a retarded schoolboy. I'm sure I sound like one. In boot camp the staff and senior volunteers told us "Take it slow in the first weeks! Don't rush in to start projects before you know what's really going on." Lord knows I'm trying, but what if the universe doesn't cooperate?

It could be a lot worse; unlike most volunteers I have the luxury of going to a work site where people use French on the job, whatever other languages they may speak at lunch break. (Kayesians speak a formidable assortment of languages besides French and Bambara, though no one speaks English.) In Bambara, as you might imagine, I'm still a little nervous about trying to communicate anything more complex than "How much for five mangoes?" As for French, apart from a bit of Rosetta Stone brush-up before we left, I walked out of my last high school French class in 1969. The Irish Christian Brothers did their work well, though, and it's amazing how much has come back, stored somewhere down there in the spinal cord alongside the Pledge of Allegiance and the Hail Mary. Thanks to them, I've been able to hit the ground walking, so to speak.

As my formal *service* (pronounced *sair-vees* like the French, and meaning our main job), I am assigned to work with Radio Rurale de Kayes, a non-profit radio station that combines good local music with news and public service broadcasting in several languages for the province's rural areas. Jihadists dismiss it as a propaganda station, no doubt, and from their standpoint they are right: woven in to all the talk about agriculture, health, current events and culture is a definite bias toward religious toleration, democracy, and self-improvement. It's a mix that is eclectic and laid back, sometimes inspiring and always *local*.

Some years ago the Radio set up a hotel and cybercafé on its grounds, partly as a community service, but also to raise revenues for the station. A big part of my assignment is to work with the internet café staff, both on the computer/technical side of things, and on the business side. Just how I do that is up to them, and me.

This incarnation of the café doesn't serve coffee. Known as the Community Media Center, or CMC, it started up just over a year ago with help from UNESCO and a talented Peace Corps volunteer, now long gone. It is holding its own financially. Pleasantly surprised, I analyzed the revenue records to find out why: Piracy! Just over 40% of the café's income is from hip young Malians discretely downloading music and videos. Probably not what UNESCO had in mind when they helped set it up, but hey – it is the financial base that keeps the café going, and three bright young people employed. From a Malian standpoint, poaching off the global entertainment industry to keep the Radio alive is most definitely a community service.

From Day One I was thrown into the deep end. A wave of virulent virus attacks on the CMC's computers had me in the driver's seat way too soon, running ragged just trying to keep the system up. I was not completely happy with that turn of events; our normal m.o. at Peace Corps is to do a gentle reconnaissance and find out what *they* need, long term, before launching into any kind of action. The last thing in the world you want is for them to be saying "Whose café is this, anyway?" Hopefully it will be fine. Once we're over this hump I've got a raft of ideas for introducing new services that won't involve pirating and will bring more women through the door – like training the smart young staff on how to create first-class resumes for jobseekers for a fee, and bringing in computer software to teach English.

The Wet T-shirt Contest

Guess what's the most fun part of my day. The commute! How many Americans can say THAT?

At full Dauda Warp Speed it's just a 20-minute trip from my house to the Radio by bicycle, but what a trip! Many's the time I've wished I could strap a little videocam onto my bike helmet to give you all a taste of it. I've been on bikes all my life, and pretty much keep pace with the hundreds of gents (and a great many women) on motorcycles. Is that because I ride at 40 mph? No, it's because nobody does. The streets, especially around the huge market area, are chock-a-block with people and machines of all sizes – big rigs out of Dakar, Chinese three-wheeled minibuses, immaculate white Toyotas with a radio mast on the hood and an NGO logo on the door, handcarts, donkey carts, pedestrians, and herds of cattle being driven down the main street to the slaughterhouse – all in constant motion, and all waiting for that fleeting moment when they can pass whatever it is that's in front of them.

The streets themselves are a long narrow battleground between commerce and traffic. Mangoes, lumber, hats, gourds, frying fish and bright plastic do-dads – row on row of vendors all trying to steal that one extra foot of space from the road. It's a roaring multimedia display of engines, brakes, shouts, jammed gears, *Griot* music blaring from dashboards and shops. Dust and diesel. A work perpetually in progress.

Traffic here is not a flow, but a series of second-by-second negotiations. As I pass the cyclist who's passing the donkey cart who's passing the old man ambling along with a cane, I make strategic eye contact with the young girl, baby on her back, waiting to cross ahead: *Not now, little sister, hold tight.* And I just have to trust that the big old truck and the *motos* coming up behind have watched me pull out and are taking care of me in the same way. Driving on roads that often look like they are recovering from recent mortar attacks, no one can afford more than the briefest backward glance.

Chaotic, yes; but it works. The road has no center-line – why bother? – and the width of each lane expands and contracts moment by moment in proportion to the volume of traffic headed in each direction. Years ago one of my old professors at Berkeley actually did a quantitative study of Third World traffic (non)management, and found that this laissez-faire approach allows a road to carry up to 30% more vehicles per meter of street width, and keep 'em moving. The crucial ingredient is *cooperation*; when that rusty old lorry piled high with cowhides comes barreling down the road in your lane, you don't stand on your rights; you stand by the roadside with your hat in your hand. Yeah, you eat a lot of Humble Pie (and sand); but tomorrow morning he will hit the brakes for you when you break out of the pack and scoot in front.

Unfortunately, there is one major player who refuses to cooperate with any of us: the sun. One stretch of my commute is a long gentle uphill grade, and I have taken to measuring the progress of the hot season by the gearshift setting on my bike. During our site reconnaissance in March I took it all in top gear; but as the morning temperatures edge into the 100s I have become a backslider, wimping down to 6th gear, then 5th, and finally to 4th gear on an afternoon visit at 110 F. That damn hill gets steeper every week.

But lately I have enlisted a new ally in this daily struggle with the cruel sun: I call it the wet T-shirt contest. If I stuff my dress shirt in the backpack and don a sopping wet T-shirt just before hopping on the bike, will it last the distance to give that precious 10 degrees of cooling, or will Mr. Sun have it dry as a bone by the time I arrive? So far the score is T-shirt 6, Sun 0. No doubt the

Radio folks find it slightly hilarious to see me strip off and transform into a sweatless bourgeois gentleman before entering the cybercafé; but better that than a heart attack.

The Apartment

We have left the Peace Corps transit house and moved in to our very own apartment, a crumbling but serviceable affair on the main road close to the crazy market scene that I bike through every day. Downstairs lies a storage room stacked to the rafters with hundredweight sacks of rice, millet and sorghum. Uh oh... The good news is that the rats are so indescribably happy down there that they rarely come upstairs to see what's for supper. As for the road, being close to the bustling market is handy; being on the truck route from Dakar to Bamako is not. On a typical day some 300 heavy lorries rumble past, morning and night, some of them massive enough to rattle the teacups. At 115 degrees Fahrenheit you can't very well shut the windows to buy some quiet, can you?

For me, the saving grace of the place is its broad flat roof, where I go in the cool of the morning to read, sip my Nescafe-and-chocolate, and gaze out onto the green swathe of the Senegal River. Green! Never take it for granted.

Up on the roof

May 2011

Dust Bowl Refugees

Late at night, after yet another dust storm had swept through, we heard a faint patter of raindrops that swelled to a roar for a few glorious minutes, leaving the air cool and sweet and soft. Well yes, the roof leaks a little and the downspout has been scientifically designed to blow the maximum tonnage of water into our little kitchen, presumably to help wash the floors. No matter; what a welcome visitor it was for a parched Hilo boy! Allah is indeed merciful, or at least has a healthy sense of humor. He slams us with four months of blistering, debilitating heat, while providing a bounty of mangos in all flavors and sizes to keep our spirits up; he lashes us with dust storms all night, then holds the sun at bay for a few precious hours next the morning (yes, real clouds!) so we won't get quite so sweaty sweeping up.

Ah, the joys of dust storms. Tiny pieces of Mali, Mauritania, and Senegal in your food, your sheets, your toilet paper and everything else, in sight or out of it. (Do clean horizontal surfaces exist in Mali? Not for long.) We are trying hard to protect the computers, but the dust gets into places even water can't go, and there are times when we can't see the river 150 meters away. For the first time I can truly appreciate Woody Guthrie's dust bowl ballads, where he wrote of rooms where the light bulb on the ceiling looks like a dim red distant thing. It doesn't surprise me to hear that respiratory problems are the second biggest health hazard in Mali, after malaria. Malaria's turn comes next month, when the rains will start to come in earnest (everyone hopes), turning the dust to mud and bugs. If not... Nobody wants to think about that.

The Dead Toubab Shop

For my money, one of the finest of the Mali volunteer traditions is the Dead Toubab, as in

"Where did you get that great Dogon shirt?"

"Got it off a dead Toubab."

Toubab (or Tubab) is short for Toubabu; in colonial times it pretty much meant Frenchman, and now means foreigner, especially white foreigner. For most Malians, it doesn't matter much what particular white country you come from; your culture, your tribe, is Toubabu. Makes sense to me. Like many ethnic tags, the word can be said with a sharp edge, or just as a moniker. In the market you may overhear things like "Toubabs don't know the price of water," meaning we are so rich, we can afford to be stupid. Ouch! On the other hand, hell, if I had a dollar for every little kid who innocently shouted Toubabu! Toubabu! as I rode past, I could buy a seat in the Senate.

But *dead* Toubabs? Most PC volunteers get off the plane with a backpack and leave 27 months later with the same pack – equally crammed, but with different stuff. What comes with are the diaries, the music, the masks, the overcoat that hasn't been worn since Boston, the technical manuals that will never be opened again, and enough clean underwear to get home. What stays behind is a cornucopia of used Malian shirts and pagnes, sandals, suntan oil, bike tools, hats, headphones, harmonicas and household bric-a-brac. Some of it, like medical supplies, is recycled, and valuable things like guitars and furniture may be sold. But the rest flows down from the villages to the Stage houses, where it piles up in old tin trunks like driftwood in the bend of a stream.

By the time a new batch of volunteers shows up on site, fresh-faced and eager to set up shop, the owners of this stuff – the Billys and Jessicas and all the Dearly Departed – are phantoms, just pictures on the wall and names in some good story told over a beer. Likely as not their gear has already been picked over by the mid-service cohort (the ones telling the stories), but the Kayes Dead Toubab trunk still held treasures for a veteran Salvation Army hound like Ms. Kanji. I have never met Mike, my predecessor at the Radio, but every night I wet down his old cotton shirt and don it like a cape to gain enough precious cool minutes to sleep. Asifa has half a dozen dresses from his wife Marisa and others, and we fire up our cooking stove with the propane tank that stood in Mike and Marisa's flat. The intimate souvenirs of ghosts. And at some level, I suppose, we hope that a little bit of their experience will rub off on us.

And what will *our* legacy be to the Newbies of April 2013? College kids now trudging off to French class, their first Peace Corps recruiter still out there in the hazy future, blissfully unaware that they will someday find themselves in a dusty little town in Africa, scrounging through David and Asifa's old stuff.

"Hey, where did you get those sandals, Bigfoot?"

"I think they're from some Dead Kennedy."

The Dead Toubab Shop de Kayes

Iced Tea, or Giant Termites in Earth Take-over Bid

How many people can say they've just spent a couple weeks hanging out with The Kennedys? That's the name our *stage* or training cohort goes by, not to be confused with Risky Business, the Hoboes, or Team America. After we'd spent two or three months at our sites, Peace Corps called the whole Kennedy clan back to Tubaniso for in-service training, or IST, or (punsters being what they are), Iced Tea.

Forget the workshops on needs assessment and accounting methods for illiterates. For me, the highlights of IST were:

a. Existing at ambient temperatures measured in two digits Fahrenheit rather than three;

b. Sleeping with a sheet actually *on top* of you (oooh, what a concept!);

c. Becoming personally acquainted with eighteen hundred thousand jillion giant termites;

d. Finding no broken bones, just broken hearts as Canada's footballers triumph; and

e. Seeing our friends return from their sites a little thinner, a little tougher and smarter, but no less enthusiastic.

As for (a) and (b), coolness in Mali comes at a price. The big rains have not yet come to Kayes, but they were in full force outside Bamako. One night, above the roaring wind, cracking tree limbs and punishing rain, a desperate cry sounded from the volunteer huts:

Allah k'an kelen-kelen wuli!

God grant that we wake up one by one – and not die en masse this night from war or natural disaster. We all smiled; it's a common good night blessing. How could Providence help but be moved by terror expressed so eloquently? And from the lips of an American Toubab at that? From all the surrounding huts came the traditional response: *Amina!* Amen.

Then came the plague of giant termites. Picture a million busy creatures with three to four inch wingspans and fat green-brown bodies, shedding their wings in gossamer carpets, chasing each other with amorous intent along the walls and floor, and eventually dying in grisly brown heaps. Malians in the remote villages love them, not for the havoc they wreak on every hut, but as a tasty, nutritious snack. For them, one of the surprise benefits of electrification has been an increase in protein intake during termite season, which falls pretty much during the hungry time of June to October. Swarming termites are attracted to light; flip the switch, and voila! You've got ten thousand delicious visitors.

On Saturday the Kennedys played host to a gang of Canadian volunteers and their Malian staff for a friendly co-ed soccer match. Tubaniso's football pitch looked like a World War I battleground after the night's rains, but no matter; the teams slipped and slid, laughed and fell, and by halftime everyone's jersey was the same color of mud. Final score: Canada's Malian staff 4, Peace Corp Malians 3. None of the volunteers on either side managed to score a point... on the soccer field, at any rate. Off the pitch it was a total rout. The Québécoise teammates were charming, and pretty, and our poor lads were quite defenseless against them. As the bus pulled away, one young swain heaved a dramatic sigh and spoke for all: "I'll never forget you, my darling Number 20!" No bones were broken, only hearts.

IST Farewell

On our last night there was a campfire, with singing and cozy conversation deep into the night. The next morning, beginning with us Kayes folks at 2:30 am, people would start making their way back to sites all over the country. This was the last time we would all be together until close of service, two years from now. I sang two songs I'd written for the occasion– La Bamba in Bambara (hey, somebody had to do it), and a short ditty entitled *Advice to Bachelors:*

> *You may not have a smooth ride in life;*
> *You may not be long in the purse.*
> *So try to marry a Peace Corps girl*
> *'Cause whatever happens… she's seen worse!*

When it came time to leave I made my way slowly around the circle, trying to memorize each face in the firelight. I know it sounds dreadfully sentimental, but I was so *proud* of them. Here they were, 60 young people living in village conditions that are just awful by any American standard, alone and unable (for now) to understand most of what was being said around them, and charged not with just existing, but with accomplishing real work. Many had to haul their bikes over five miles of rough roads at 110 degrees just to buy a tomato for Pete's sake, because their home villages are too small to have a market.

Listening to them talk, there was none of the hip, detached cynicism that we have all grown used to at home. Plenty of gallows humor, to be sure, but no whining. It was as if someone had taken my very best students over the past ten years – the ones with both brains and courage – and had planted them around the fire.

June 2011

Gainful Employment

We're back in the bustling work-a-day world of Kayes, after two weeks of IST in the bucolic training center at Tubaniso. Outside my window the metalworkers across the street are banging and clanging to beat the band: John Henrys with 9-pound hammers in the noonday sun. A young boy of about 12 wanders by, dressed in a tattered rag that proudly proclaims in English, "This T-shirt would look good on your bedroom floor." Innocence squared. Teams of laborers load enormous sacks of rice and millet onto an ancient wood-sided truck that sits patiently by the road like an old donkey. A minute later, all of us are eating dust from a procession of proud, sleek 18-wheelers out of Dakar. The joint is jumping! No doubt about it, it's fun to sit in the shade and wax poetic about other people's hard work.

But hard work is just what's in store for us in this next phase of our service. With the end of IST, the settling in period is over. It's the start of Get out there and Do it.

I'm ready... I think. A couple weeks ago I sent out a strategy memo to the Director of the Radio that outlined some ideas for making it and the cybercafé more sustainable. As it stands, the Radio is financially healthy but has limited sources of income, so it has had to rely heavily on grants from NGOs (non-profit groups) for anything that requires a substantial chunk of money. UNESCO, for example, bought the computers for the cybercafé. NGOs are great, but it's dangerous to become too dependent on them. They come and go, and have their own priorities. Listener-supported radio is more sustainable. Problem is, the countryside around Kayes is very poor, and unlikely to generate much hard cash no matter how loyal the listeners may be.

On the other hand, the Kayes region is famous for its *tunkeranke* – the Diaspora of tough emigrants who have left their hard-scrabble homeland and made a life in Europe, the Arab world or North America, much like the Cantonese of China.

So part of my proposal to the Director was to use the Radio's new on-line capabilities to cultivate this diaspora as an extended audience of overseas listeners and financial backers. The Radio is going digital over the coming months, and this is the perfect time to create a modern website that will allow people to listen directly over the Web, or to download their favorite radio programs whenever they want. They can call in or be interviewed 'on the air' virtually free via Skype... and so on. In any event, the roll-out of the new website and listener services should be done in conjunction with an advertising and fund-raising campaign targeted to the *tunkeranke*.

The long-term goal is to create a set of loyal overseas Malian supporters, people proud of their roots and willing to help the Radio's work whether or not they actually listen much themselves. The short-term goal, and the first fund-raising effort, would be to create an independent water supply for the station and its internet café and hotel spinoff operations. Radio Rurale stands at the edge of town; although it is connected to the city water system, the supply is irregular and extremely expensive by Malian standards. By drilling their own tube well, they can cut their monthly operating expenses by ten to fifteen percent, which would allow them to salt away some cash every month to pay for new equipment or make it through financially lean times. The problem is to find the 4 million CFA (about $8000) that it would take to build the well without going into debt.

Eight thousand bucks is a lot of money in Mali. If the Director hoped that Peace Corps might foot the bill, he's in for a disappointment; that's not the PC way. For the Kayes Diaspora, on the other hand, $8000 is an entirely do-able fundraising target...

As for the cybercafé, it is doing fine financially but has wandered off the path of community education and service that UNESCO envisioned when setting it up. So for them the trick is to find new ways of doing community service that will enhance the Bottom Line as well. Among other things I'm going to be training the staff in advanced Excel and other Office programs, and will teach them how to create resumés for clients; both are good Peace Corps-ish activities, but won't rake in much money.

Then I thought of Rosetta Stone! Almost no one speaks English here, even educated folks, but there is a huge need and desire for it. I test-marketed Rosetta Stone English at the café using the company's on-line demo, and it sparked enormous interest. Unlike music videos, it will be a genuine community asset. It seems that nobody in the whole province is doing adult education in English. So my first project for the café is to write Rosetta Corp and see if I can get a donated copy. The program is very expensive, and the café really can't afford it on its own without charging extortionate prices to users, which defeats the purpose. If that fails, I'll try to scare up other sources of funding, or go with one of Rosetta's competitors.

When my Peace Corp boss Adama came out to visit Kayes, he and I had a great 45-minute session with the Director. Monsieur le Director had read my memo closely and was very enthusiastic, as the plan dovetailed with a number of other things the Radio was planning to do. A good start all 'round. As for the reality of how it all turns out? I'm way too old and jaded to expect it to unfold neatly and sweetly; for one thing, we don't know yet how many of the Diaspora have internet access. For another, the Radio staff will have to get off their butts and take on some new tasks – and many of them are verrrry comfortable with things just the way they are. But that's all part of the journey. Stay tuned!

Inside the CMC

What's in a Name? Joking Cousins Revisited

Dauda Coulibaly & Fatoumata Diarra

What's in a name? A rose by any other name would smell as sweet… but not a Diarra.

Nearly everybody in Mali takes part in the Joking Cousins tradition. Malians come into the world fully equipped with a set of prescribed 'cousins' marked by particular family names, or sometimes whole ethnic groups. They will tease and be teased by these people for so long as they both shall live. The custom goes back to at least the 13th century, when it was popularized by the great Mande emperor Sundiata Keita – the historical model for the Lion King story, some say – as a way to diffuse tensions between rival families and ethnic factions. That same easygoing spirit continues today: cousin jokes may be silly, and are often

185

stereotyped, but they are never genuinely nasty. Even some things that would strike us as mind-bogglingly rude to say to someone you have known for all of 37 seconds ("you are my slave," for starters) are recognized by all as stock lines from an ancient playbook and are jovially paid back in kind. It's a wonderful tradition, and deserves much of the credit for keeping Malians a sane and mellow people.

Fair enough you might say, but how is it that foreigners get roped into mandatory fart joke duty? The short answer is that they don't, unless they take on a Malian name – which is precisely why all Peace Corps volunteers get one early on. No name, no cousins, no fun. Most PCVs get Malian names during their early language training in the villages, and the first or given name is usually something Muslim. I chose the local equivalent of my American name, as King Dauda is a well-known figure in the Koran. You'd be surprised how many people have Old Testament names in the Islamic world: Daudas, Miriams, Bacharies (Zachary), Yacubas (Jacob), even Issas (the prophet Jesus) abound. The Founding Fathers and Mothers of Islam are another big source of first names, as chronicled in the holy book and filtered through African languages and French spelling: Mamadou (Mohammed), Alfouseyni, the Prophet's wives Kadiatou and Fatoumata… To our Malian friends Asifa is a Fatoumata, as I am a Dauda.

But it's the *jamu* (surname) that is most important part socially, as it determines your joking-cousin allies and adversaries, and conveys lots of other information besides. Many names are more or less associated with a particular ethnic or linguistic group, of which Mali has many, and volunteers usually take on surnames consistent with the African language they learned during home-stay. Coulibaly and Diarra are both common Bambara names. It's the biggest single ethnic group and the most widespread of the languages. Coulibaly and Diarra are also 'noble' names, as opposed to Caste (i.e. former slave) names. A Coulibaly dynasty ruled large parts of Mali 300-400 years ago. The legendary ancestor of the Diarras was a brave and compassionate warrior who found a wounded lion, approached it unarmed, fed and nursed it back to health.

Of course, having a noble name has nothing to do with present realities. The best Western analogue of Couilbaly would be the Scottish Campbell or Stuart, old royal names now claimed by people who are commoners by blood. Unlike the ancient Scotts, though, Malian surnames are not really clan names in the anthropological sense; they don't refer to real units of social organization. The closest they come to being 'clans' is in joking cousins, where all the Coulibalys, all the Diarras and all the everybody else's are treated as unified tribes for joking purposes. There is an intricate, country-wide weave of these ties.

No one takes it seriously. I mean, I am pretty obviously not from around these parts, but no one, ever, has questioned my inherent Coulibaliness, or Asifa's fundamental Diarrativity. It's all a game, and part of the game is to pretend that it's not. It's as if everybody in the US were born with a sports team as their last name, and some teams are ritual arch-enemies. If America had joking cousins….

Scene: The Holiday Inn, Evansville Indiana. The bar.

"Pleased to meet you. How's the family? Saw you in the seminar. Pretty good presentation, eh? What's your name?"

"Dan."

"What's your team?"

"Yankees."

"Yankees! Poor guy! Don't you get tired of eating donkey meat?"

"I find it quite nutritious. What's your team?"

"Dodgers. Art Dodgers. Good to meet you, Dan. Yeah, I wondered what that smell was. I can tell you're fond of Mexican food."

"Now Art, you know that young boys shouldn't talk so freely with their elders."

"True enough, but your mother never taught you that slaves should know their place?"

-And so on. They will find these jokes familiarly hilarious. And when they tire of the game, Dan the Yankee will say "Go Dodgers!" and Art the Dodger will return with "That's me! Go Yankees!" And they'll go on to have a normal adult conversation, having broken the ice without ever once mentioning the weather. Now if that isn't Civilization, I don't know what is.

Bambara

Gather 'round, trainees! Lesson One:

I ni sɔgɔma!	Good morning! (lit. You and morning!)
Mba [Nse]! I ni sɔgɔma!	Untranslatable man's [woman's] response! You and morning!
Hɛrɛ sira?	Night was peaceful?
Hɛrɛ dɔrɔn.	Peace only.
I ka kɛnɛ, wa?	You are fine/ healthy, yes-no question indicator?
Tɔrɔ si tɛ.	No troubles at all.
So mɔgɔ bɛ di?	People of the house are good/ sweet?
Tɔrɔ t'u la.	No troubles come to them.
K'an b'u fo.	Good-bye! (lit. We greet them)
U n'a mɛn.	Good-bye! (lit. They hear your greeting)
Ka tile hɛrɛ caya.	May the day's peace increase
Amina!	Amen.

Daunting, isn't it? What you are looking at is pretty much my first glimpse of Bambara. It's a much-shortened version of the greeting conversations that you, as a well-mannered person, will have with just about everybody you meet during the day. Even if you can't say anything else in Bambara, you must know how to greet and bless; it shows that you are at least trying to respect Malian ways, however clumsy and... well, foreign, you may be in all else you say and do.

It's so important, in fact, that Peace Corps sent us some dialogues like this before we ever set foot on Malian soil. Being busy with packing, I just stashed 'em on my Kindle with never a second look. When I finally opened them, it was in the dead of night at 37,000 feet somewhere between Paris and Bamako. See the Sahara scroll by in the moonlight far below. See Uncle David. See his jaw drop and forehead wrinkle. Holy moly! It was not just the funny letters that I had no idea how to pronounce; or the contractions, or the grammar, which seemed way more opaque than any I had come up against before. What struck me most was the utter strangeness of the way normal, everyday things are said. "They hear your greeting" means goodbye?

Then the moment passed. "Hold on," I said to myself. "Utter strangeness? Look again. Good morning. Did you have a good night? How's the family? Give them my regards. Have a nice day. This is basic, human stuff. We are all one species, after all. You can hack this."

We're all one species, but we sure talk different. Mali has 13 recognized national languages (plus French), and not one of them is universally understood. Bambara comes closest, as a first language for about 30% of the people, and a language that you can get-by-in-if-you-have-to for another 50%. Bambara is part of the Mande family of West African tongues which (some scholars say) began to split off from the southern Bantu languages some 7000 years ago. Linguists disagree on just how to classify the

Mande group in the broader scheme of languages and this makes them very happy, as it gives everybody a wonderful excuse to fly off to Florida for conferences. What can't be denied is that Bambara and its cousins have virtually nothing in common with the Indo-European family, whose speakers conquered the world from Ireland to Russia to India in the old days, and invented just about every language most Westerners ever hear.

I have never studied Japanese or Hawaiian, but I expect the shock is similar. If you take up Spanish or Swedish or Serbian, even Hindi, there will always be that comforting Ah-Ha! sense of meeting old friends – words, or rules of grammar – in new costumes. Some of it is due to recent borrowings, to be sure; you don't need a Ph.D to figure out where *le weekend* comes from. But the family resemblance goes much deeper than that, largely because it is, literally, a family. All the Indo-European languages descended from a common ancestor that was spoken maybe 3500 years ago, and the common heritage of words is astounding: Kinship, body parts, pronouns, animals, time, motion, numbers, the senses. Snow, fire, life, death; and hundreds more words that share the same roots. It's also true, to a lesser extent, for grammar. Yet even if we know all this intellectually, we take it blithely in stride when studying our sister languages. Mi, ma, min, mio, meus, men, meine, mene, meri – somehow it all seems perfectly *natural* that they all mean 'my', doesn't it?

Then there's Bambara, where *ma* means not, *mɛn* is to hear, *mɛnɛ* to light, *mɛri* Town Hall, and *min*... Well, *min* can mean where (as in Where is the bathroom?), to drink, and three or four other things. Common heritage? All bets are off.

Mind you, Bambara does have some redeeming qualities for the linguistically challenged. For one thing, the nouns don't have gender. Hurray! I never did get used to the logic that says a French cup is feminine but a glass is masculine; or worse – that wine is masculine, but beer is linguistically girly. How many hours of my precious youth did I waste memorizing stuff like that? Bambara, like English, applies gender only to things that *have* gender, and then it just slaps on -cε or –muso at the end, from the words that mean man and woman. So you'll have jakumacε (catman) and jakuma*muso* (catwoman). Very practical.

Another great thing is that the sounds of the language are pretty easy to handle. A volunteer in Namibia may have to tackle languages with as many as four different click sounds, each as different to the natives as thin, fin, and sin sound to us. In Bambara there is nothing more exotic than the ŋ and ɲ sounds (ng as in Sing and ny as in Onion), and the occasional Mb or Ns at the beginning of a word. The funny ε ɔ vowels that seemed so scary at first are just soft versions of the e and o, as in *sent* and *song*. Piece of cake! Best of all, Bambara adopted the International Phonetic Alphabet as its writing system in the seventies, so words are spelled exactly as they sound. If you were a native speaker, I could stand here and read you a book from cover to cover without having the faintest idea what I was saying. But you'd know. Pity the poor Malian student who was raised in the luxury of Bambara spelling and must now take on the insanities of French or English!

That's the good news, which they always tell you first. The grammar is something else. For starters, I want you to meditate on 'to have,' in the sense of possession. It's an unappreciated little workhorse that we use 63,000 times a day, and it doesn't exist in Bambara. The concept exists, of course, but is expressed as something being near or with you:

Moto bɛ bɛnkɛ Dauda bolo.
Uncle Dauda has a motorbike. (Don't I wish!)
[Motorbike is uncle David hand.]

This expression draws on the word for hand; it can mean that something is literally in your hand (unlikely in the case above), or simply that you own it. Likewise,

Nɛgɛso bɛ n fɛ. *I have a bicycle.*
[Iron-horse is me with]

Iron horse! Isn't that, like, a totally cool word for bicycle? And if you interchange the object for the subject, the meaning shifts from 'have,' to 'like' or 'want.' In the hardware market...

I bɛ mun fɛ? N bɛ nɛgɛso fɛ.
What do you like/want? I want a bicycle.
[You are what with? I am bicycle with.]

You can see how things might get confusing in some situations, especially since Bambara doesn't have words for 'the' and 'a.' Take

Wùlú fatɔ bɛ Charlie fɛ, for example.

This can equally mean 'Charlie has a rabid dog,' or 'The rabid dog likes Charlie.' Both could be true, of course.... Speaking of dogs, you see the little accent marks in wùlú? Those are tone markers. Bambara has two or three tones, depending on how you count it. Most words don't require tones, so we greenhorns haven't gotten much into that yet. Like English, Bambara is a lingua franca used by millions of people who don't speak it well, so native speakers will cut you a lot of slack in the pronunciation department.

But for virtuosos of the Joking Cousins game, tones provide some of the finest opportunities for Gotcha! moments. Some of the most famous ones play on the subtle difference of tone between *wùlú* (dog) and *wúlú* – a man's Throbbing Python of Love, shall we say. Given the grammatical switcheroo that is possible between 'have' and 'like,' it's not hard to imagine a joking cousin waiting for just the right moment to casually observe, "Oh, I see you like a little dog!"

Ahem. Moving right along. The hardest part of Bambara for me is the particles – the legions of *la*'s, *ra*'s, *na*'s, *ka*'s and *ye*'s, which I swear are scattered at random across most sentences like chocolate sprinkles on an ice cream cone. Here are some simple *ye*'s:

Ne **ye** wolontɛri **ye**.   *I am a volunteer.*
[I   **<attribute marker>**   volunteer   **<attribute marker>**]

An **ye** nin kɛ Asifa **ye**   *(Sounds like pig Latin!)*
We did this for Asifa.
[We   **<past marker>**   this   do   Asifa   **<for>**]

The particles are shape-shifters. For the most part, they don't actually mean anything in themselves. Instead, they help to set up grammatical structures that make other words mean something, and how they are placed can alter the whole meaning of a sentence. Trouble is, these same over-committed little words are enlisted in a hundred different structures, and you can't get what's being said until you grasp the structure as a whole. Got that? I wish I did. It's my greatest downfall in conversation. If I miss a *la* or a *na* or a *ye*, a whole sentence can become mush. And as I try to figure that one out, more sentences whiz by until I'm standing like a grinning fool, buried up to my neck in tiny words. For want of a nail, a shoe was lost; for want of a shoe, a horse was lost....

For all my clumsiness in learning to speak it, I still think Bambara is a splendid language. Eskimos may have 26 words for snow, but how many languages have words for different kinds of shade? How many have three distinct layers of color terms, the most ancient with only black, white and red, a second based on the colors of healthy grass, shea nuts and manioc leaves, and a third stocked with *orange* and *rose* and other exotic imports from French? How many have the poetry to speak of the humble bicycle as an iron horse, for that matter, or to say Welcome! with a word that descends from the Arabic invocation 'In the name of God?'

Aw bisimila!
Welcome in the name of God.

July 2011

Don't just Plan there, Do something!

We're still on the Appetizers course of the rainy season, featuring occasional visits by punchy little storms that don't green up the landscape much but do keep the dust down and the humidity up. Though we are definitely in two-digit territory on the Fahrenheit scale, the Comfort scale is sliding back as the air (and the insides of our sweaty clothes) fill with moisture. Nobody pays much attention to the lack of drainage except the mosquitoes, who are grateful and send little thank-you notes to the Mayor's office from time to time. On the bug front, the locals tell us *You Ain't Seen Nothing Yet.*

At work, July was the month when the planning stopped and the doing really started. Scary! I took a deep breath and started a series of mini-courses for the CMC staff on Microsoft Office, beginning Leçon 1 with Excel. Although they have all had some catch-as-catch-can experience with Office, we're going step by step to show how they can go about training other people.

My three young charges are all about 23 years old, and all very fine folks. Yacouba Sissoko, the manager, is an affable man with a ready smile, and with the tawny face and light skin that around here signals Arab ancestry. His family comes from Kayes Ndi on the other side of the river, where they run a small shop selling motorbike parts. The Radio is a big step up for him. Yacouba is looking for a wife these days, and the quest has spawned 'Project Sissoko,' an ongoing farce in which the rest of us pair him off with impossible women. In return he explains, with much disdain, how they could not possibly be good enough for him: Celine Dion? "Too noisy; she would never let me sleep in on Saturdays." How about Madonna, then? "Too big, too hungry. She would never let me *out* of bed."

Souley (Souleymane) is a quiet young man whose parents are farmers. Serious and steady, he was the first to be hired when the CMC opened. Souley is intensely proud of his fiancée, a nice girl who studies in a distant town. One day he took me aside to confess what he could not tell the others, that he dreamed of saving up enough cash to open his own cybercafé in a place close to where his family lives. I felt honored.

Bintou is in many ways the most interesting of the CMC trio. Forthright, chic, intelligent and as tall as the boys, it was Bintou who was favored for the manager's slot when the café was starting up. The Director quashed that idea tout de suite, saying (so I am told) that she had the bad habit of saying precisely what she thought. That would never, never do for a woman manager. She teases constantly, and there is a warmth to it. "Souley, if you don't stop mooning over your girlfriend, you will trip over those ridiculous feet and break something." Unlike the boys, Bintou is passionately curious about the outside world. I love her for it, but sometimes it breaks my heart. One of the exercises in our lesson book is to set up an inventory system for a French restaurant. I chatter on about Excel formulas, oblivious to the fact that she has no idea what half the items on the menu are. What is a salmon? We get on the net and I show her one. What does lobster taste like? What's a chalet? Tell the truth now, you have actually seen a whale? She has never seen the sea.

I have done a lot of teaching, but never in a foreign language: "See, you just cliquez sur le button Fat in la barre de utilities 'Put It en Forme', and Voila, les étiquettes will appear plus grosses.[4] C'est simple!" No, my French isn't really that awful, and we're using some very well-crafted materials put out in French by Microsoft as a public service gesture. Language is always a challenge for me, but less so in the small, bounded world of technology.

The technical stuff is the easy bit. The hard part, if you are coaching future coaches, is changing habits of mind that people don't know they have. Though the café staff are very bright and very motivated (lessons are all done outside regular work hours), they have never learned to *play* with technology, and that slows them down. I'm working with Sissoko on some new Excel techniques that will help them streamline the accounting system:

"... OK, we've just created a drop-down menu for services. Let's make another one for prices."

He freezes.

He knows what to do – he's just done it – and the spreadsheet has been working fine so far.

"What if I make a mistake, and it all goes *détraqué* (haywire)?"

---

[4]Just click on the Bold button in the Format section of the utilities bar, and the fonts will look fatter. It's simple!

"Just jump," says I. "It'll be fine."

Where their techie counterparts in America would plunge in and immediately start pushing buttons and pulling levers – exploring, tweaking, experimenting: hmmm, what does this do? – these young people are far more cautious. Is it a kind of reverence, or maybe a fear of bringing Microsoft Office to its knees if they do something rash? No doubt their school experience has a lot to do with it; Malian schools are big on rote learning and mindless repetition.

But it might run deeper than that. North Americans and Europeans grow up surrounded by smart machines of all sorts, every minute of the day, to an extent unimaginable by most Malians. And so we (well, many of us) tend to be fearless with our electronic servants, as experience has taught us that much of what we do *is not really real*; the Undo button will save us. Malian young people have spent most of their lives in a world populated by people and animals, not machines, and certainly not data machines. In that world actions have consequences. It's hard to find the Undo button on a goat or a friend. Just a thought.

Bilingual Money

You'd think money would be one of the easier things to master in a new place – "a mark, a yen, a buck or a pound" and all that. There are big currencies and small ones, but they're all cut from the same decimal cloth, right? Right.... and then there's the CFA.

Mali doesn't have its own currency. Many years ago it decided (quite wisely) to team up with a bunch of other West African countries to form the Central Bank of West Africa and issue the franc Communauté Financière Africaine, or franc CFA (pronounced 'say-faa'). If currencies were people, the CFA is the little guy in a shabby suit whom everyone pretends not to notice at the bankers' party. Next to the CFA, a Polish zloty looks positively muscular. Microsoft Excel, which offers 407 currencies to choose from, snubs it. On the other hand, there's an upside to having one's money designed by a multinational committee: it's pretty. Colored a pleasant red, green or blue (when not too dirty), the notes are festooned with cheerful and forward-thinking airplanes, trains and antelopes, iconic African masks, and amber waves of grain. Not a single dead politician to be seen.

So why do I call it 'Bilingual Money?'

That's the interesting part. The CFA uses two completely different counting systems, depending on what language you are speaking. Not just different words that refer to the same numbers, but *entirely different numbers*. If you are speaking French, it's straightforward; the numbers you talk about are the same numbers that appear on your bills and coins. The banknote says

'2000 CFA' and you say "Here's two thousand." Not in Bambara! Handing over that same banknote to a Bambara speaker you would say, natural as can be, *Kɛmɛ naani file:* "Here you go! Four hundred." What gives?

Bambara and the other African languages have perfectly good vocabularies for expressing numbers. The trouble is, they don't count money the way they count everything else. The number *kɛmɛ naani* means four hundred soldiers, kilometers, or bags of rice, but two thousand if you happen to be talking about CFA.

When you talk money in Bambara – to quote a price, pay, bargain, or make change – it's understood that your numbers refer not to CFA but to *doromé*, a unit of money which doesn't really exist, but is nonetheless equivalent to 5 CFA. It's not just in Mali; you'll find oral accounting with doromé all over French West Africa. How did this strange situation come to be? Nobody seems to know for sure. The best guess is that it hearkens back to the Moroccan *dirham* or the Spanish *peseta douro* (five-franc piece in gold) that were carried across the Sahara by Arab traders. The numbers on the coins changed, but the way people talked about them did not.

For the Westerner used to calling a buck a buck it produces a bizarre kind of sensory disconnect, especially if you are actually looking at the invoice or at the banknotes you plan to pay it with. The actual coin says 100 francs, but if you are speaking in Bambara you'll refer it as a *mugan* (twenty). When the fruit-seller wants *bi segin* (eighty) for that bag of mangoes, she doesn't mean CFA; she means *doromé*. So you fork over 80 times 5, or 400 CFA.

Bizarre it may be, but the weirdest part is that it actually works! For anything under 5000 CFA (meaning 90% of the things we buy day to day), Asifa and I usually prefer to be quoted prices in the African system. For me, it's more straightforward when talking in Bambara. The trick is to 'Africanize' the way you think about the CFA, by learning the doromé value of each kind of banknote and coin. That way you can convert Bambara prices directly into cash, bypassing all that dreary multiplying and dividing by 5.

Another little advantage for Americans is that the exchange rate of CFA to dollars these days just happens to stand at about 500 to one, which makes a doromé just about equal to a penny. That makes it dead easy to translate Malian prices into American ones if we are ever tempted to do that.

And let's face it: how great is the competition? I'm just a country boy, but I reckon any language that needs to say *dix-huit cent quatre-vingt quinze* (eighteen hundreds, four twenties and a fifteen) for 1895 is no great leap ahead of Bambara.

Pop Quiz! What is this man selling? Answer on page 211.

August 2011

I'm Dreaming of a Green Ramadan

August was a month of praying and waiting. The big, proper rains have still not come, and the locals hope and pray that they will be late rather than missing. Even so, the sky gods have been generous enough to keep us busy mopping floors and bailing out the balcony, which becomes a mosquito factory after every little storm. My theory is that this house was built during the hot season. "Drainage holes?" said the builder. "Why bother?" Plenty reason: even in this dry year we are seeing the usual surge of rainy season diseases. Cholera has broken out between Gao and Timbuktu in the east, and several volunteers have come down with malaria, including one of our good friends in Kayes. So far we have been spared anything serious on the disease front... but keep bailing, Uncle David.

Long stretches of my morning commute have also become more interesting as I and 14,000 other bikes, motorbikes, cars and trucks each plot our own strategies to ride anywhere *but* the road, parts of which are under water for days at a time. I shudder to think what it would be like in a year of heavy rains! In this, as in so many other things, the Malians are pretty hopeless as Fixers, but are cheerful and gracious Copers. We speed up, slow down, drive on the wrong side, communicating with the merest of gestures, sharing what little high ground there is. Want to learn something about Malian values? Come take a ride with me.

This year August was the month of Ramadan, a time of reflection and fasting for Muslims. Although people still go to their regular jobs, they take no food or water from sunup to sundown. At work my colleagues did get a bit sleepy in the afternoons, and the soft drink machine was unplugged for the month, but everyone took it in stride. Growling stomachs and parched mouths notwithstanding, most folks are cheerful and mild. Even the nicotine addicts – of which there are many among Malian men – sigh philosophically and wait for sunset. Allah has cooperated with relatively balmy weather this time around, but Ramadan is a lunar fast and moves backwards through the calendar year by year. Not so many years from now it will come during the searing 120° F / 50° C heat of Kayes in May, and I wonder how the faithful will cope. As for Asifa and me, we did eat lunch and kept ourselves hydrated, but always in private. No one expected us to fast.

Although the days are austere, the nights of Ramadan have a special cozy feel as families turn inward to break their fast together. It is a time for reading from the Koran or listening to radio preachers, patching up old quarrels, giving to the poor. And like the Christian Lent, Ramadan ends with a joyful bang: the feast of Eid Al Fitr, started by the Prophet himself so they say, not long after his flight from Mecca to Medina to escape assassination.

And remember when you were few and were reckoned weak in the land, and were afraid that men might imprison you; but He provided a safe place for you, strengthened you with His help, and provided you with good things so that you might be grateful. [Koran 8:26]

Powerful sentiments there; shades of Passover and Thanksgiving.

On Eid day Asifa and I were invited to celebrate with our friend Moussa and his family in Kayes Ndi, a three or four mile walk to the far side of the river. We set off mid-morning, dressed in our very finest Malian gear, Uncle David awkwardly hiking up his long *boubou* against the mud and the dust. Got to look respectable, you know. It felt like Easter morning, the streets full of smiling people looking splendid as can be and exchanging jolly greetings with total strangers. How could we resist? We *Eid Mubārak!*-ed and *Aw sambe sambe!*-ed our way through the market and across the bridge.

Eid Mubārak!

At Moussa's we sat down to a fine festive supper, starring charcoal-roasted mutton and *capitaine*, a large river fish stuffed with fragrant greens. I must say, it was the best damn meal I ever had in Peace Corps, served up with love and the all-out generosity that is so typically Malian. But feasting isn't really the point of Eid Al Fitr; in between prayers at the mosque, Moussa took us around with him to call on neighbors and friends, paying his respects, catching up on news of the family, and exchanging blessings special for the day.

May this be our first feast and not our last.
May your life be as solid as an iron bar.

May worms not alter it, nor termites.
May God have pity on the departed.
May God accept our prayers.

-Each good wish answered, of course, with a fervent *Amina!* Kids, too, had a field day, dressed in their holiday best and going around the neighborhood in small flocks of friends to beg for sweet rice cakes. The grown-ups give them blessings and a small treat. It reminded me a little of Halloween, maybe, or English wassailing, but less rambunctious.

Dressed in their holiday best

As we headed home from celebrating this second-greatest of Muslim festivals, the strangest thought popped into my mind: *Bring Back Lent.* "Where did THAT come from?" I asked my brain. Then I thought about it. Of course: Lent is in many ways the Christian Ramadan.

When you strip away the religious trappings, Ramadan and the traditional Christian Lent are really the same idea – a mass spiritual exercise, a time of sacrifice and renewal that the whole community takes part in. Picture a world where, for one month out of the year, *everybody you know* sets out on that same journey, to take stock of who they truly are and how they treat the people around them, and to rise above the discomforts of hunger and thirst. A month when people are conscious of trying to be good. It's a discipline many of us in the West have never learned; but, like jogging, it goes better if you do it in company. Islam does it on a global scale.

Christmastime is the closest our culture comes to a mass spiritual exercise, I suppose (not counting Superbowl), but we have turned Christmas into a season of indulgence and not much else, and given up on the austerities of Advent. That's a pity, because the shared self-sacrifice of a Lent or Advent creates opportunities for soul-searching that just don't seem to happen when we are too comfortable, or do it alone. We have lost the centuries-old tradition of using the run-up to Christmas and Easter to make ourselves better persons.

So here's what I was thinking as we walked back over the bridge, bellies and hearts full of Eid cheer: Thanksgiving is the best of our North American holidays. It celebrates no military victories, no revolutions and no particular religion, though it is at home with all religions. How much more joyful would Thanksgiving be if the whole week leading up to it had been set apart by tradition, like Ramadan, as a time of fasting and reflection? And if *everybody* did it?

Don't push the River

The veterans call it the Six-month Blues. You're still struggling to make friends, cope with the living conditions, have something that resembles a real conversation... and you have to face down thoughts like "Can I really accomplish *anything* in a place like this?"

One of the keys, I'm finding, is to just relax and let things unfold at their own pace. A Malian Peace Corps staffer said to me early on, "We Malians use time to meet our needs. For you Americans, Time uses *you*." Not very elegantly put, but there's a lot of truth to it. Much, much more than Americans, Malians live in the present. It's one of the main reasons why they are so poor, but also so happy in spite of being poor. Yes, it could lead to disaster some day, especially if they keep making babies at the present rate; nobody seems to be thinking too seriously about that. I guess they'll cope with the new situation when it arrives.

One of the great things about Peace Corps life is that – on one level at least – it is so very simple. No house repairs; no gardening, car repairs, phone trees, no setting up automatic payment protocols for a thousand and one bills. I have spent many years as a consultant, and this feels for all the world like being on one great big fat 27-month site visit. All the normal cares of normal life are left behind; instead, you are constantly faced with new sights, new tasks and people. Your stripped-down life frees you to focus on that new experience, and on the work at hand.

Best of all, it frees you from the prison of Toubab Time. Lately I've found that if I relax a little and let some of the Malian sense of time seep in to me, I accomplish almost as much but with a lot less stress. We are in a strange mental space here: on the one hand, everyday living conditions are probably the toughest we have had to deal with long term in any of our travels. On the other hand I feel freer here than I have felt in many years, even in Hawaii, and much freer than during the career-building years in California and Norway. I have time here. Deadlines are flexible and self-made, and if they don't work out, as often happens, everybody is easy about it. -Including me, if I let myself. That's the hard part, of course.

I'm just beginning to realize at a gut level how much of my life has been ruled by anxieties over deadlines large and small. Mind you, I don't regret the past at all; the whole ride has been fun. And I'm sure that here too there will be times when it is not like this, and I'll be up against the press of events and have to hustle. That'll be good too, to bring back that old Dionysian thrill of riding the wave and pushing to the extremes. But for now I'm enjoying the quiet space created by a world that operates on flexible time, and in the long run it may help me understand better what makes Malians tick. How can you have such a hard life and be so cool about it? This might be a piece of it.

August 2011

D&A Go National

Not long after I wrote that last essay, about how nicely strange it was to have a life not crammed with deadlines, the Fates took notice and said "We've got to do something about that boy."

Out of the blue I got a call from UNESCO (the UN's educational, scientific and cultural agency) in Bamako, which runs the Community Multimedia Center program for all of Mali. The project ends in December – they're turning it all over to a government agency – and they want some help coming up with performance indicators, final training sessions and an exit plan that won't lead to the 23 CMCs dying on the vine in a year or two. They even offered to pay me $3000! Of course PCVs can't accept a dime for anything, but the work still needs to be done.

From where we stand in Kayes, it's pretty clear that the UN administrators in Bamako have not been paying much attention lately to the problems of CMCs on the ground. This transition period may be the last chance for CMCs to voice their concerns and have some input into the future shape of the system... if we're lucky. Peace Corps has been cooperating with UNESCO for many years, and is happy to see someone dive into the breach.

So, with Asifa fast becoming the Jeannie Appleseed of Moringa, it looks like we will both be spending more time in the capital over the next few months. I hadn't really expected anything like this to happen in our first year of service, but what the hell; it's the sort of thing we enjoy most.

The everyday work in Kayes goes on. The CMC staff are about to graduate from their Excel course, complete with certificates and a little party. (Oh how Malians love their certificates!) After six weeks of silence, Rosetta Corporation wrote back to say that they don't do donations anymore, so I'm applying to the Peace Corps Partnership program for a small grant to bring English teaching software to the café. The Radio folks are very excited about it, and think the demand will be enormous.

Well, there you have it: even if you don't push the river, you'd better be ready to swim.

PS- Answer to the 'What is he selling?' picture quiz: You are looking at a gas station for motorbike riders. Customers buy their petrol one liter at a time, served up in recycled French Pastisse bottles. There are three regular gas stations in Kayes, and 50 or 60 of these little stands. Moto riders like the convenience, nobody shuts them down for safety violations, and 50 more people have work.

September 2011

Water

Water is never a sure thing in this part of the world. Pull up Google Earth and fly to Kayes, and you'll see what I mean: vast khaki-colored plains, fading to deep desert as you head north. Kayes is just a tiny dot by the river. This is the Sahel.

The name was given by Arab traders centuries ago, and means 'the Shore' – the shore of the desert, a gigantic band of dry savannah skirting the Sahara from the Atlantic to Sudan. Even in a normal year there is virtually no rain for nine months; then come the blessed weeks from June to September, when the clouds roll in and dump most of the year's quota for this area, a scant 18 inches or 50 cm, in short, violent storms. The Sahel would hardly be populated at all were it not for the inland Niger delta, Lake Chad, and the Senegal river valley (that's us). In the big scheme of things, even these regions are just oases on a vast scale, kept on life support by water imported by Nature from other places.

This has not been a normal year. We have had rain, but not enough of it, and we are nearing the end of what should be the rainy season. The clouds roll in, drop a tantalizing five minutes of real rain or a pathetic piddle of drizzle, and move on. The days unfold hot and humid, as the sun takes back the little moisture the clouds have given.

For us urban folk, the drought has just been a minor annoyance so far. Cuts in the water supply have become more frequent, and the thick, cloudy iron-tinged stuff that comes out of the taps is very different from the clear water of April. Fortunately our 20 liter Peace Corps-issued dual filtration system has been equal to the task. Although we have to add chlorine now for the first time since our bootcamp days in Baguineda Village, we have never had to go without drinking water. Bath and laundry water? That's another story. The cuts come pretty much at random, with no warning and no idea how long they will last. On Saturday we got caught flat-footed with barely two quarts/ liters of water to last us from 9:00 in the morning until 11:00 at night, when the taps finally began to flow again. You can imagine the pair of us, salty, stinky and cranky, first filling every vessel in the house and then luxuriating in long, cold, midnight showers!

For the farmer and herder, though, every drought is a potential death threat. Mali went through two horrible droughts, in the 1970s and mid-80s, that killed 40% of the country's livestock. According to USAID the herds will probably never recover completely, and many pastoralists have been forced to turn to marginal dry-land farming. Historically, most droughts in this part of the world have been regional and not quite so devastating, though I reckon that's small consolation if you are caught in one. To the north the desert is expanding, and with global warming all future bets are off. Our bushwhacking missionary friends say they know farmers north of us who have already given up on planting this season, and their prayers these days all include that ancient invocation to the Almighty: "Lord, send us rain."

Travels with Vacher

Rain or no rain, Asifa and I had planned to spend our 36th anniversary weekend at a lovely riverside spot called Manantali, complete with bellowing hippos (yes, really!) and some tumble-down huts that volunteers use as an R&R center... But duty and meetings called, so instead we headed off for the two-day journey to Bamako on the Peace Corps shuttle. The shuttle is a venerable institution in Mali: half a dozen sturdy white Toyota Land Cruisers plying the roads on a more-or-less regular schedule from the capital to our far-flung posts and back, carrying medicines, mail, manuals, and as many volunteers as will fit. Slower than the express bus, but a lot more fun.

Our driver was Vacher (Cowboy), the steadiest, fastest and at times most daredevil of the PC drivers, and an institution unto himself. He's my age more or less, lanky, crusty, kind, and the best damn driver in the fleet. The driver makes a big difference, especially at this time of year. The shuttle has many errands to run on the way to Bamako, and takes the long route via Bafoulabé, Mahina, Manantali and Kita. It gets wetter as you go south and most of the way is unpaved, so long stretches of it have become an endless series of deep mud puddles. Get caught in one of those in the middle of nowhere, and you've got yourself a problem.

We headed southeast from Kayes on a brilliant Friday morning, all green grass, red road and smooth sailing. This first leg is the new Chinese road – unpaved, but 60 feet/ 18 m wide, graded, and with modern conveniences like bridges and culverts. While we Americans provide mosquito nets and set up HIV/AIDS programs, the Chinese are building infrastructure to extract Mali's gold and other resources. They know exactly what they want. But hey, they sure can build roads! Vacher gunned it on the long straight stretches and we found ourselves doing 105 kph (about 65 miles per hour), my personal record for a dirt road.

The Bafoulabé ferry

Near Bafoulabé the Chinese road peters out, and we waited a while for the little car ferry that would take us across this stretch of the Senegal river. Once across we delivered some malaria meds and a propane tank to one of our fellow volunteers in the village, then headed down the muddy rutted road to Mahina. A tire gave out at that point, but the Road Gods were kind and we were able to get it repaired at a little shop in the town.

Even so, the flat had put us a good hour behind schedule, and late is not something Vacher likes to be. Rather than head back ten muddy miles to the car ferry, he made a sudden left as we approached the tall narrow railroad bridge at the edge of Mahina. But...but... ! Plip, plop went two wheels of the Toyota, as we placed ourselves half between the rails and half on the little walkway that flanks the tracks. Off we went, bumping along the railroad ties. The Bafing branch of the Senegal river is a good half mile wide at this point, so there was plenty of time to discuss the American custom of flattening pennies (and other metal objects, such as Toyotas) under the wheels of trains, the fantastic stories our friends could tell around the dinner table once the news of our spectacular demise got out, and so on, all the while enjoying a fine bird's eye view of the river. Vacher knew the passenger train schedule by heart, and just grinned like a kid picking apples from the neighbor's orchard. Nothing coming by here for hours. But freight trains? Wellllllllllllll– not two minutes after we had reached the other side and plomped off onto the service road, a big mother freight came rumbling past down that one and only track. All in a day's work for Mr. Vacher.

After a brief stop in Manantali to pick up some volunteers and deliver more med supplies, we dodged yet another 100 km or so of mud puddles and spent the night in the PC Stage House at Kita. The Kita area has a lot more volunteers than Kayes, and we spent a jolly evening drinking beer and catching up with old friends. The next morning we were off for the easy three-hour jaunt to the capital, on roads that were actually paved.

Bamako was a blur of activity for both of us. I met with the UNESCO staff, consultants, and the Peace Corps Mali Director on ways to ease the transition of the CMC network into the tender arms of the Malian government, while Asifa held a flurry of meetings on her 'Plant a Seed' project to integrate Moringa awareness into Peace Corps training and activities throughout Mali. Most nights we slept double-bunked and eight to a room in the Bamako stage house, a warren of unwashed dishes, Simpsons on the wide-screen TV, and raging 23 year old hormones.

As for our 36th anniversary, it fell on Labor Day, a day when all Americans in Bamako cease to labor. So we did the ex-pat thing, lounging around the pool at the American Club, drinking cold beer and getting to know some volunteers we had never met before. Later in the week we rested from our hard work and blew an estimated 11.3% of our entire September living allowance on a very fine meal at Comme Chez Soi, a gracious little restaurant and B&B run by a spunky young couple from North Carolina, of all places. Salmon (!), pork (!!), and home-made ravioli were on the menu, with Malian Key Lime Pie for desert. How in the world did they ever wind up in Bamako, not to mention getting hold of salmon and pork? Buy me a good glass of wine sometime and I'll tell you all about it.

November 2014

The Peace Corps and the Marine Corps

Like US embassies everywhere, Bamako's has a small contingent of Marines to guard the gates and handle other security jobs. We're not supposed to fraternize with them. It's not like the Peace Corps sees Marines as a bad moral influence or anything; they say it's because hanging out together will provide raw material for the never-ending rumors that portray Peace Corps volunteers as covert military or CIA. "That's a laugh," you might well say. "What in the world could a steely-eyed jarhead and a dewy-eyed PCV possibly have in common?" On the surface, not much; but dig a little deeper and you might be surprised.

There's the obvious stuff, of course. Both services are made up mostly of young, fit people. They work for the US government, promote American interests, and wind up in obscure out-of-the-way places that nobody has ever heard of, all over the world. Granted, Marines and Peace Corps volunteers tend to do slightly different things once they unpack their rucksacks...

No, the real similarities lie in the nature of Peace Corps and the Marine Corps as *organizations*, and particularly in the way they inspire loyalty, sacrifice and performance in their people. How do they pull it off?

One big part of it is a clear sense of purpose. I have always been struck by how intensely Marines as individual men and women seem to embrace the Corps' mission as their own. I'm not a veteran – dear Mr. Nixon ended the draft just before I finished college – and I never quite understood that kind of commitment, not in my gut, anyway. Since joining Peace Corps, I get it.

A Marine's mission is to fight the enemy. Human beings being what they are, it is immensely helpful to have an enemy, some palpable person or thing or idea that threatens what we hold dear. Who was it who said, "Nothing so powerfully concentrates a man's mind as to know that he will be hung in the morning"? Enemies do that too, rightly or wrongly; they free us up to concentrate on the *how* of removing the threat, bypassing the enervating uncertainties of *Should I?* Do Peace Corps volunteers have enemies? Sure they do: malaria, malnutrition, ignorance, helplessness. And when you combine this with the Agincourt effect – 'We few, we happy few, we band of brothers' (and sisters!), standing up against enormous odds – you've got a recipe for unrivalled esprit de corps. Come to think of it, what's the Marine motto? "The few, the proud, the Marines."

Ideas like that rattled around in my mind for some time in a vague, back-burner kind of way, until somebody sent an article from *Forbes* that put it all into sharp focus.[5] John Greathouse is an entrepreneurship guru, and the bottom line of his article was to deliver an important message to managers of start-up companies, namely: "Love Ain't Free, But It Can't Be Bought." You can't buy your way to the kind of loyalty and creative initiative that will make a start-up blossom. Not even with employee stock options, free snacks and on-site dry cleaning. What you can do is to create a culture where employees are motivated by a shared sense of purpose, and by a commitment to the organization's mission. What would such a culture look like?

Let's look at two cash-strapped organizations, he says. Each has established an enviable track record for attracting, motivating and keeping good employees, despite some of the most extreme working conditions you can imagine. What do they have in common?

Organizational Characteristic	Marine Corps	Peace Corps
Sense of Purpose	High	High
Mission Clarity	High	High
Group Identity	High	High
Educational Opportunities	High	High
Personal Fulfillment	High	High

[5] John Greathouse, "Go To War With Your Competitors: Fight Like The Peace Corps." *Forbes Online*, February 11, 2014. http://www.forbes.com/sites/johngreathouse/2014/02/11/go-to-war-with-your-competitors-fight-like-the-peace-corps/.

Ability to make an Impact	High	High
Cash Compensation	Low	Low
Equity Participation	None	None
Performance Bonuses	None	None

A key element in the esprit de corps of both groups is that they see themselves as part of an elite organization of high achievers. They take pride in their toughness, and that pride helps Marines and PCVs put up with things that sane people would not. As for educational opportunities, both organizations will help their people get into later college or post-graduate studies, but that's not the main thing. Greathouse:

> Both organizations enable members to gain life skills they can utilize for the remainder of their professional careers. Both corps learned long ago that people learn and grow profess-ionally when they are given the chance to solve problems on their own, rather than follow a recipe... Not everyone will thrive in such an environment, which is why hiring autono-mous, self-directed individuals is especially important...

Autonomous, self-directed individuals in the *Marine Corps?* You bet. Of course the Corps has ranks and a top-down chain of command; all armies do. What distinguishes the modern US military – as opposed to the Malian army, for example – is that soldiers of all ranks are trained to make tactical decisions on the ground if the situation demands it. The strategic decision to Take That Hill will probably be made at headquarters; but precisely *how* to take that hill will be determined by commanders at the scene and, in smaller ways, by each soldier responding to opportunities as they present themselves. It's not so different in Peace Corps, really: the principles of PEPFAR and PMI, America's strategic AIDS and malaria initiatives, are handed down from Washington and filtered through the administration of each Peace Corps country. As grunts on the ground, it is our job to adapt those principles to the local terrain and make it work in our villages. Both services value people who know how to take the initiative.

And that, says Greathouse, is one of the best ways to make a low-paying, difficult job more rewarding. Plonk your people down in an environment that challenges and stretches them; allow them to take on as much responsibility as they can effectively handle. Give them some guidance, and a mission. Then give them room to reach their personal potential as they pursue that mission. Self-education and crucial life skills will follow.

Asifa and I could see this process working in a young colleague posted in the southern part of our province. Years ago some NGO had installed tube wells to bring clean water to her village, but the pumps were broken, and no one could repair them. There was one working faucet for 1000 people. The men did nothing about it; after all, it wasn't they who now had to wait for hours to fill the family bucket. Our friend's solution was both brilliantly simple and (from a Malian standpoint) shockingly audacious: train the *women* to repair the pumps! It's just not done, said the men, but the women were all for it. Peace Corps Bamako supported her all the way, and in the process she learned how to negotiate with the village powers that be, put a project proposal together, and get it funded. Multiply this story by ten thousand

and you'll begin to see why so many Peace Corps veterans come back stronger people.

But to know that you personally are learning and growing is not enough; to stay motivated on $10 a day, you have to feel your work is accomplishing something. Most volunteers do feel that way, although it's more like fighting a guerilla war than a nice tidy battle where, at the end of the day, you can measure the ground that's been captured. If you're lucky you'll be able to stick around long enough to see your projects take off and fly. If you are not – and that's distressingly common for all kinds of reasons – you'll have to content yourself with the gospel preached by senior volunteers during pre-service training:

Any project that is big enough and good enough to have a long-lasting effect will take time. It is better to lay a firm foundation for local people and future volunteers to build on, than to rush through projects that don't have local buy-in and rely on lots of outside money.

Even if you are a conscientious volunteer, you may never see the results of your work. And in the long term you CAN never see the results of your work. Your greatest effects will happen indirectly, through the people that you lived and labored alongside, and influenced in some way. All you can really do is make sure those influences are positive.

And we did see the signs of those untraceable long-term effects, especially in Ghana, where Peace Corps has been doing its thing for 50-plus years. Time after time, we would meet a technician, scientist, teacher, manager, entrepreneur, community activist, and learn that there had been a Peace Corps volunteer in that person's life. Someone who inspired them, probably without even knowing it. "Her name was Jane. She came from the middle of

America, someplace near a river. She was the first one to teach me about science. If I knew how to find her, I would write a letter to say thank you." Are there people who feel like that about the Marines they have known? I can't say.

As for compensation, if you find a Corpsman or Peace Corps volunteer laughing all the way to the bank, it's not for the obvious reason. Both services do offer small end of service payouts, and extra points if you apply later on for a government job. As a line on your resume, it sets you apart from the pack. Food, health care and housing are covered. But that's not what recruits are thinking about when they sign up. For the Marines, as Greathouse points out, a big draw is the chance to play with some of the most expensive toys in the world: planes, tanks, weapons systems straight out of a Bruce Willis movie. The kind of gear that can cost as much as the Peace Corps budget for an entire country.

Peace Corps volunteers aren't even allowed to ride a motorbike. On the other hand, we get to hang out in wildly exotic places and live day to day alongside the strange people we serve. Perhaps most important, we know that at best, we will build something that's good and lasting; at worst, we will do no great harm. For my money, that's the greatest inducement of all. *Everything we do is positive.* Maybe that's why you will never hear a returning Peace Corps volunteer say, "I don't want to talk about it."[6]

---

[6] Though their core mission is indeed "to kill people and blow stuff up" (as one former jarhead described it to me), I'm not implying here that Marines do nothing but destroy. In fact, during the Vietnam era it was the Marine Corps that pioneered the Combined Action Program (CAP), in which squad-sized units were sent to live in Vietnamese villages. As well as organizing the local militia for defense, they provided medical support for civilians and did civic action projects such as building schools, offices, and wells. It's the closest the Marines ever got to acting like Peace Corps volunteers, and in

December 2011

Normal

It has been a very busy few weeks here in Lake Kayesbegone, though not exactly the stuff of great storytelling. Toyota-flattening freight trains, giant termite attacks and the like have been in short supply, and in recent days even the weather has mellowed down to something that could mostly be called comfortable. This I can handle. What worries me more is that some of the everyday craziness of life here – trading fart jokes before you buy an onion, saying "Here's two hundred" as you hand over a banknote that has One Thousand written all over it, even the exuberant potholed death-defying chaos of my daily bicycle commute – it's all starting to seem... well, Normal. Yes, yes, human nature and all that, we can get used to almost anything and not even realize it. But another part of me is going Nooooo, this is Peace Corps! I didn't sign up for Normal!

When you take something for granted, how much do you lose? Oh Lord, hear our prayer. Keep us fresh. Deliver us all from Normal.

---

fact CAP was one of the models for later Marine and Army counter-insurgency operations in Iraq and Afghanistan. Check out John Southard's *Defend and Befriend: The U.S. Marine Corps and Combined Action Platoons in Vietnam*. University of Kentucky Press, 2014.

Walking the Walk

On the other hand, a dash of Normal now and then does help you get a lot done. For both of us this has been a very intense but satisfying time in our service. Asifa spent much of November at the Peace Corps training center in Tubaniso, doing sessions on Moringa and project management for the Goodfellas (the *stage* sworn in this summer) and the yet-to-be-named new group who arrived at the end of October. I have been bouncing back and forth between Kayes and Bamako, and was with Asifa at Tubaniso to help with some of the orientation sessions and welcome the newbies as they arrived, shell-shocked, from the airport. It's hard to believe that they will be sworn in as full volunteers this time next month. Pre-service training seems so long when you are in the midst of it, but viewed from the outside it flashes by in a heartbeat.

Mostly I've been working with my Community Media Center here in Kayes, and with UNESCO as they struggle to hand over responsibility for Mali's 23 CMCs to the government. The UNESCO staff have become more harried and disorganized as the project approaches its end, but I must say they have tried to be responsive. They really appreciate Peace Corps being involved, and actually incorporated most of the suggestions we made in designing the four final training conferences for CMC directors and managers. As for the government agency that's taking over, I'm trying to be optimistic, but I have my doubts. Suffice it to say that the muckety-mucks show up without fail to have their pictures taken for the press, but we don't see much of them otherwise.

In the end self-reliance is what it's all about, and the Kayes operation will be fine. Thanks to a Director who is honest and entrepreneurial, and great groundwork by an earlier volunteer, Kayes has come to be regarded as the New York Yankees of the CMC world – venerable, profitable, well-organized, and always innovating. So UNESCO asked us (with a week's notice) to play host for the third training conference <u>and</u> to make a presentation on our Excel-based accounting and recordkeeping system. Yikes!

Sissoko, Souley, Bintou and Coach Dauda worked long hours in the short time we had. For the presentation, the biggest challenge was conceptual – getting them to recognize just how much practical knowledge they already carried in their heads, and distilling it step by step, slide by slide, into a form that everyone could understand. On the other hand they took to PowerPoint like a hippo takes to water, and showed a fine natural ease and frankness as speakers once they had convinced themselves they could do it. When the big day finally came I just stood in the back and smiled as my three protégés held the floor for over an hour, fielding questions and later coaching the assembled CMC Directors through a hands-on exercise. They were the youngest people in the room by ten years.

The crowning glory of the event was a distribution of computer software for teaching English through voice and images. Every CMC in Mali got a copy. Since I was the only one who'd had any real experience with the program, I ran the session on how to install and use it. My fractured French probably made their ears hurt after a while, but no matter; at least for now, everybody is infatuated with Madame Anglais.

The Toughest Client You'll Ever Love

In the midst of all this, my dear wife roped me into the most fun project I've done since coming to Mali. Her Plant a Seed initiative on Moringa involved creating zillions of different materials, including several PowerPoint presentations and pictorial animations (since most village people can't read). I was helping out a little on the computer side. Then one fine Sunday afternoon she cornered me in the kitchen and said the fatal words "Dahling, I've been thinking." This, as we all know, is the married-people code word for Trouble.

"Yeeessssss....?"

"We need a song."

"You want me to write you a love song?"

"A Moringa song. We need a song to get the volunteers all fired up about Basiyirini."

"You want me to write a love song to a _tree_?"

"If an Irish Coulibaly can't do it, who can?"

She is my most difficult client. And she doesn't pay very well, either. But who could resist an assignment like that?

The Muse-goddess of Semitropical Vegetation must have been eavesdropping on our conversation, because the song practically wrote itself. I brought a notebook and chair up to the roof, gazed out on to the river and a gorgeous sunset, and in an hour it was done. The tune is Waka Waka, an old West African song that had been tweaked with some English verses to become the theme song of the 2010 World Cup. Everybody in Mali, from old folks to street kids, knows the tune and the chorus. The parts in English got new words, and the chorus parts in the Fang language (tsamina mina zangalewa etc.) were replaced by simple catchy Bambara phrases. Voila!

Basiyirini Waka Waka[7]

[To the tune of Waka Waka / This Time for Africa]

Watching the kids run, feeling the stillness
Joy you can see, 'cause they are free from hunger and illness
We're on the front line, we've got to make sure
That it will be; the Miracle Tree is part of the answer
It helps you grow – you feel it!
It helps us all – believe it!

Bana kunben, ka fisa
It is better to prevent sickness
Ni bana furakɛ ye
-Than to treat it.
Bana kunben, ka fisa
It is better to prevent sickness
A de bɛ se ka kɛ!
It can be done !

---

[7] Waka Waka (This Time for Africa, sung by the Columbian singer Shakira), was the official song of the 2010 World Football Cup held in South Africa. It is based on a West African song, *Tsamina mina Zangalewa,* that has been around for at least 40 years. For more information on the fascinating history of the Waka Waka song (not all of it completely accurate), see
http://en.wikipedia.org/wiki/Zamina_mina_%28Zangalewa%29.

Basi yiri ni, a ka nyi
Moringa is good stuff;
Waka waka hey hey
Get it done, hey hey !
Basi yiri ni nafa ka bon
Moringa is important
A de bɛ se ka kɛ!
It can be done !

Planting and selling, cooking and growing
Do what you can, we've got a plan to get where we're going
We've got the power, we've got a chance here
If we can see the Miracle Tree is part of the answer

Today's the day – I feel it!
We pave the way – believe it!

Bana kunbɛn, ka fisa
Ni bana furakɛ ye
Bana kunbɛn, ka fisa
This time for Africa

Basi yiri ni, a ka nyi
Waka waka hey hey
Basi yiri ni nafa ka bon
A de bɛ se ka kɛ! / [This time for Mali-la!]

But how to get people to learn and sing it? Easy: Since it was the
World Cup song, there HAD to be a karaoke version out there
somewhere. I found a good one, added a guitar track in the Radio

Rurale studio, and did a rough demo version to show how it could be sung. Volunteers sang it 'live' as karaoke at Asifa's Moringa training sessions, and it was recorded by some fellow volunteers who actually know how to sing. Most Malians can't handle the English verses, but they picked up on the catchy Bambara bits from Day One. Nowadays when I come in to the Radio or we visit Peace Corps HQ in Bamako, we are greeted with an ebullient chorus of Waka Waka from the staff and security guards – and I hear that a young woman from Baguinda village (our homestay site) has taught it to a youth group. What fun! The next step is to do it as a dance video.

Then what? Although Asifa's and my projects have mostly been separate, the timing has been amazingly parallel and we'll both be winding down this phase of our service soon. I've got to serve on some kind of sustainability panel for the CMCs, and Asifa will be presenting her Moringa work at a conference near Dakar, but then it looks like we're back to being homebodies for a while.

Christmas Cheer

Hey kids, here's a special Christmas treat!

Though I can't imagine why, the good people of Kayes seem to be having a hard time getting in to the Christmas spirit. So to help out, I tried my hand at creating some culturally authentic local carols…

♫ *The holly and the ivy*
Have gone out for a walk
In the Kayes Sahel there's nothing there
But dirt and sand and rock. ♫

♫ *While shepherds washed their socks by night,*
All seated on the ground
Tabaski[8] came and all the sheep
Were killed and gobbled down. ♫

♫ *Frosty the Snowman*
Didn't last very long in Kayes
And the children came from miles around
Just to watch poor Frosty die. ♫

Hmmmm. Can't put my finger on it, but my carols don't seem to make people all that *jolly*. Well, it's the thought that counts. Merry Christmas, everybody!

February 2012

Well I'll be Dogon

Help, I'm turning Malian!

It's freezing. Not literally, but cold enough to make me crouch at my desk at noon in a wool hat and fleece wrap that last saw the light of day in Washington DC. Never thought I would be able use the words 'freezing' and 'Kayes' in the same paragraph.

---

[8] Tabaski (Eid al-Adha) is a Muslim holiday that involves eating prodigious amounts of mutton.

We've had a blessed three-day cold snap, caused by an enormous dust cloud that rolled down from the Sahara to cover all of Mali and most of its neighbors. Last night we cuddled under our Peace Corps-issued Refugee Blankets (yes, really; the same ones they use in UN refugee camps). Today the sky is a bright silver bowl of fog and dust. The river, just 150 meters away, is a ghostly shadow, and the east wind whips through our big unglazed kitchen window. People scurry by in hats, shawls, and heavy jackets cast off by all the Salvation Army stores of Europe. Tomorrow the town may be back to its usual steamy self, but as for today... do I *really* have to take a cold shower?

We're back in Kayes after our first official vacation in Mali, a trip to Dogon country in the east. Dogon! The natural habitat of all those exotic masked dancers, stilt walkers, cliff dwellings and hairy sorcerers you see on the tourist posters. We had to go see for ourselves.

It's another world, even for most Malians. The people look a little different – less Arabic influence maybe – but that's not the main thing. It's just that... Let's put it this way: like some native Hawaiians, the Dogon people live quite happily with two very different operating systems installed in their heads. They say that Dogon is "30% Muslim, 30% Christian, and 100% animist." Below the layer of Christianity or Islam is a whole other world of nature spirits, old, old practices, and magic. That hut over there is where women go to avoid polluting the village with their menstrual blood; those monkey skulls embedded in the wall are from sacrifices. Are humans ever sacrificed, as of old? "Not often, and certainly not in the open, but yes," Tiémoko told us.

Usually the victim is a marginal person from another village; he or she takes magically tainted food or drink, and slowly dies.

It was in Bandiagara that we hitched up with Tiémoko, a lanky late-forties Dogon homeboy who spoke a pocketful of languages and was never to be found without his broad black hat. Tiémoko is one of the vanishing Old School of Dogon guides, intensively trained – point to a tree or shrub and he can tell you its Latin name – and dead serious about his profession. His mission for the week was to lead us on a hiking trek through the heart of Dogon country.

Mesa Verde? Dogon.

The setting is no less remarkable than the people. Most of Dogon's villages are strung out at the base of the Falaise de Bandiagara, a sandstone escarpment 400-600 feet (130-200 m) high that runs through the Sahel for 150 km, or nearly a hundred miles. The cliffs are crenellated with caves, outcrops, nooks and crannies of every description, and in those crannies the ancient Dogon – and their even more ancient predecessors the Tellem – built cliff dwellings to protect themselves from attack. Shades of Mesa Verde? Absolutely. And the Tellem, they say, could fly.

There aren't many roads, and we preferred to watch the country unfold at a walking pace, step by step. We started out in Digui-bombo, a village at the top of the escarpment, where I had a most jolly time swapping a bowl of pipe tobacco with the old guys of the village. Bambara doesn't get you very far in Dogon country, but most of the older generation speak French. And unlike most of Mali, pipe smoking is very common among older Dogon men: presto, instant rapport! They smoke a mild golden leaf that is home-grown in their gardens, and it seems my navy-cut Virginia – sailors' tobacco – gave them an unaccustomed jolt. Final judgment: "A tobacco for bulls and elephants."

"A tobacco for bulls and elephants"

As we groped our way down the steep escarpment from Digui-bombo we were often overtaken by young girls with colossal baskets balanced on their heads, skipping down the narrow trail look-Ma-no-hands. What must it be like to make this run in August, when the cliff sides are a tangle of greenery and waterfalls, and rocks that have been worn smooth by a hundred thousand bare feet turn slick and treacherous? Down on the plains we linked up with two PCVs working in the area, comparing notes over goat stew at one of the *Campements* that have been set up for travelers to eat and rest. It was a somber lunch.

"The rains hardly came this year, and the harvest was only a fraction of what it should have been," the volunteers said. Kayes region has been among the hardest-hit, but it was only then that I truly appreciated how badly off some other parts of the country were. Everywhere we went we heard tales of crops dying in the fields, and grain already beginning to sell for double the normal price. The traditional 'hunger season' – the time just before the rains, when the new crop is being planted – is still months away. Malians are not prone to complaining, but there was a real current of fear here.

Dogon country has been hit by a double whammy: not only has the harvest failed, but the Tourist crop has dried up as well. On top of the kidnappings by Al Queda and its bandit contractors, the Tuareg minority in the North has once again begun to assert its demand to carve Mali into two states, with parts of Mopti province (home of the Dogons, among many others) being included in the Tuareg portion. Dogons have about as much in common with Tuaregs as Asifa and I have with the Chinese. For decades the Malian army has held them back, but this year they have reappeared in brigade strength with seasoned fighters and heavy weapons lifted from the Libyan struggle. Even in death Mr. Gaddafi is stoking the flames.

Whatever happens militarily, it has been a grand economic victory for the Bad Guys. The tourists have followed their governments' warnings and stayed home. This is supposed to be tourist high season in Dogon country, but the clean, well-run Campements were empty except for us. The sculptures and beautiful cloth sat on the shelves. We saw only two other foreign tourists the entire time. Many families literally don't know where their next month's meals will come from.

And who is to blame for all this? Omar, an earnest young man of about twenty, came up to me after our lunch break, when the local volunteers had gone off to paint a mural. Omar knew the answer.

"Obama is to blame for this. Obama and Sarkozy [the French President]. They are the provocateurs. Gaddafi was good to Mali; he gave us money, built schools and health centers. You hunted him down and killed him, for oil."

Peace Corps volunteers are not supposed to talk politics, but I couldn't let him walk away without a response.

"No," I said. "After 40 years of Gaddafi, millions of Libyans were risking everything to get a democratic form of government. They asked for our help. Americans believe in democracy, they really do."

Then tell me, he said, "What good is your democracy when a man's children are dying of hunger?"

I hope to heaven there are not many more like him, because his mindset reflects a complete propaganda victory for the insurgents. Our suffering is your fault. We talked, cordially enough, for a good half hour before it was time to head down the road. He didn't budge an inch – I didn't expect him to – but maybe that conversation with a genuine American helped to plant some seeds of doubt. It's the best I can hope for.

After a long dusty trek along the base of the escarpment, sunset found us in Teli, a tiny village in the shadow of an ancient cliff city set high in the rock. That night we joined every last man, woman, kid and dog in Teli to crowd around a snowy little TV set and cheer on Mali's Finest in the Africa Cup. All in vain, as our hopes were ground to dust by powerhouse Ghana. Damn! Of all the people on the planet, these folks needed *something* to crow about... but it wasn't going to happen tonight.

Early the next morning we scrambled up to the cliff dwellings built by the Dogon ancestors and the long-vanished Tellem people. Truly an African Mesa Verde, and a place of powerful ghosts. Even I could feel it, a sense of quiet murmurings beneath the silence of the place – helped along, no doubt, by the baboon

skulls and animal teeth embedded in the rock by generations of sorcerers and animist priests. Not the place for a midnight stroll!

We finished up at Ende, a village famous for its wood carvings, and spent a lazy afternoon with an old sculptor friend of Tiémoko's. His work is masterful in the way it brings out the living spirit of the trees it is shaped from, and he totally got it when we talked about the tradition of *akua* (gods or life-force) in the wood art of far-away Hawaii. Living art was the theme of the day, it seems, and we got a mega-dose of it at the Ende weekly market just before heading back to Bandiagara and what passes for civilization. Picture an acre of gracious old shade trees, and beneath them hundreds of market women and their customers laughing and flirting and decked out in their very best rainbow finery. Doggonit, *this* is West Africa!

You want to trade birthday stories? My 61st was spent perched atop five fragrant tons of onions. We were headed toward Mopti, an old river town on the Niger, when the *bashé* (communal taxi) broke down not 15 minutes out of town. No matter; with the driver's help all eleven passengers managed to hitch a ride on a passing truck piled high with dried onions. Nestled comfortably among the sacks we felt like well-perfumed Lords of Creation, surveying the countryside from our perch 12 feet above the road.

In Mopti we crashed with a Kennedys *stage*mate, hiked out to see his fishponds project at the edge of town, and waited out the afternoon heat under the trees, drinking 300 cups of tea and chatting with the workers. Never one to lose an opportunity to constructively yank people's chains, Asifa tossed out essay questions to the all-male crew: "So how come Malian women do all the work while the men sit around drinking tea?" and "If you had only three babies instead of seven, wouldn't it be easier to educate and feed them?" I must say they took it manfully, with grudging respect for the feisty old American lady who held such radical opinions.

The next day we hired a *pinasse* (that's French for 'gondola on steroids') for a sunset river cruise on the Niger. Our boatman was a real Bozo. No, that's not a put-down; fishing and rivercraft are professions dominated by the Bozos, one of Mali's most distinctive ethnic groups. In fact Mali is the one place on earth where you can walk up to a big burly fisherman and say "Sir, you are a veritable Bozo among Bozos," and he will thank you for the compliment. Mind you, among the Dogon and their other joking cousins, Bozos do not exactly enjoy a reputation for intellectual brilliance. Just two days before, we had been treated to a hilarious half hour of nonstop Bozo jokes told by Tiémoko and his sculptor pal. Picture every Polak, Newfie, Irish, Swede, Belgian, or Sardarji joke you have ever heard in your life... That, to the Dogon, is your basic Bozo. As you can imagine, they were just tickled to death to hear that Ameriki, in its great wisdom, had conferred that very name on its favorite clown.

Cruising on the Niger

March 17, 2012

The Four-Minute Warning

It's hard to celebrate St. Paddy's Day when you're the only Irish-man (well, sort of) for a hundred miles around. If the Senegal river is green this morning, I assure you it's for other reasons.

The winter, such as it was, is history. The big rains never came, and heat and hunger are with us again. Temperatures are back to three digits, and in the villages the food security situation worsens little by little, day by day, with rising prices and chronic shortages in some areas. Kayes province, never far from the desert, has had a particularly hard time of it. Villagers are beginning to pack up and move to the towns.

Here in the city things haven't changed much yet: city folks have money, and much of what we see in the market comes from Senegal and other far-off places. We do see signs of the troubles, though, and signs of a response. While on the road a couple weeks ago I heard an ominous rumbling behind me. Jumping off the bike, I stood by the roadside to witness the longest procession of trucks I have ever seen in this truck-crazy town. Forty heavy lorries coming out of the west, some with Senegal plates and others with the markings of Groupe Toguna,[9] all with *UN World Food Programme* placards plastered hastily on to the driver doors. Thank you, taxpayers, wherever you are.

Although the UN, US, the European Union and the Malian government have all been hustling to get food relief in place for the coming hunger season, it's still not certain that they will succeed in getting enough emergency supplies, in time, to the right people. The other, scarier question is whether farmers will have the rain, the seeds and the money to plant for next year. Our Kayes crew hosted a regional volunteer conference earlier this month, and the main theme was how PCVs can lend a hand in the coming crisis.

---

[9] Mali's largest agricultural company. They do a lot of work with USAID.

In the meantime Asifa and I carry on with our main services. Over at the Radio I'm helping them launch an English Club and develop radio commercials for our new language software. Bintou, ever the most outgoing and ebullient of the CMC staff, stepped up to the plate to write and perform a set of commercials in French and Bambara:

Hello people of Kayes! Did you know, the CMC is the place for learning English! Come to Radio Rurale de Kayes, where we put in your hands an advanced software for learning languages by means of images and sound. Come in for a free trial lesson, and join the world community of English speakers: school was never like this! We await you with impatience. See you soon!

Though I handled the recording and editing for this first go-round, it was for her to pick out the background music. I was very curious to see what she would choose, and lent her my iPod, with its thousands of songs from two dozen countries. The winner? Bruce Springsteen! From *Born to Run*.

"Have you ever heard of this guy?"

"No. Why, is he famous?"

"Very. Why did you choose it?"

"I don't know; he is strong. He has energy. He moves forward. It sounds very English."

Well, there you have it. The Boss as ambassador for the English language. Somehow I don't think he will mind.

In the recording studio

We have now passed the midway point of our service, and for me this whole month has been filled with a strange sense of end-of-the beginning. Like some cosmic referee has just given the four-minute warning for halftime.

Because at precisely 1:05 a.m. April 24 (Insha'Allah), we're off into the Friendly Skies for *Ameriki,* shamelessly escaping the worst of the hot season; and when we return it will be to a different house, far from the rumble of traffic. Our service will evolve too, though at this point neither of us quite knows how, or in what direction. We both have plenty of plans, but only a year more to pull them off.

For now, here are some musings.

Pith and Vinegar: 25 life lessons we learned in Mali (With thanks to Monica Jeannormil)

1. There is no such thing as a clean horizontal surface, or a vertical one for that matter. Sweep, or be buried alive in the sand.

2. Mangoes are God's consolation prize for the hot season.

3. French fries are a condiment. (That's right; you'll find them in your hamburger nestled alongside the catsup and mustard.)

4. Malians don't hear music unless they want to, and *can't* hear music unless it's over 100 decibels.

5. Writing is a suitable replacement for violence – usually.

6. Unless you are the driver, the trip will involve way too many people sitting way too close to you.

7. Teflon, plumber's putty, Tupperware and electrical tape are foreign words that mean little black plastic bag.

8. Being comfortable with boredom is an essential skill; learn it or die.

9. La Vache Qui Rit (French Velveeta) is an essential Malian food group. Can't live without it. Bacteria won't touch it, which is proof of their superior intelligence.

10. You can only get a hot shower when it's over 98.6 degrees outside.

11. Yes, you can miss rain and the color green.

243

12. Just because it's fried doesn't make it taste better... Who am I kidding? Of course it does.

13. Care packages are a reason to go on living.

14. Meat and fish only need to be refrigerated in America.

15. 85 degrees is cold; 75 degrees is freezing.

16. Patience can be learned, especially if the alternative is a prison term.

17. "Donne-moi cadeau! Donne-moi cadeau!" (Give me gift!) ... It's not the heat that gets you, it's the cupidity.

18. You can work up a sweat by simply being.

19. Air conditioning is a powerful bribe.

20. Warm beer is better than dirty water, but not by much.

21. Driving a motorbike is a right; knowing how to drive is a rare privilege.

22. Ice is a fond memory, kind of like Christmas ornaments, or cheese.

23. Kids can be the high point of your day and still annoy the hell out of you.

24. Friends, family, and humor can get you through just about anything.

25. Even if hunger is staring you in the face, be nice to people. Dance.

March 22, 2012

Coups de feu,[10] Coup d'état

As Asifa boarded that last fateful plane out of Bamako, I was turning out the light in our Kayes flat and settling in for a steamy, restless night. *Here we go for another hot season.* Our crazy fellow volunteers were already making plans for a "Cinco de Kayes-o" celebration, calling in PCVs from all over Mali to gather on May 5 and party hearty through the hottest days of the hot season in the hottest town in Africa. Come on out and suffer in style! Ah, Les Kids. Fortunately, we old fogeys would be far, far away, off to fabled Ameriki for a cool six weeks' holiday…

That pleasant future melted away on the night of March 21-22. Unbeknownst to any of us out here, there had been an overnight

---

[10] Gunshots

coup d'état in the capital, and the democratic government of Amadou Toumani Touré (ATT), the gent who lent us his palace for swear-in, was thrown down and replaced by an ad-hoc military junta. The sun came up on a whole new world. Here's how it looked from where I stood in our dusty town near the western border.

It's a strange thing, this modern world; due to the time difference (and uncensored media), some of my American friends knew about the coup before I did. My first memory of that morning was the phone going off at 6 am. Asifa? No, it is a Hawaii friend calling to ask what has happened. *What do you mean, what has happened?* I reassure her that it is just another of the demonstrations that are being staged by elements of the military these days to protest President ATT's handling of the Tuareg insurrection. It is an honest answer, as that's all we in Kayes are aware of at this point. Back to bed.

At 8:00 I am awakened again, this time by the sound of gunfire all over town. It starts from the southeast, where the military barracks are (not far from the Radio), then from the southwest, where the main road comes in from Senegal, and finally from the market area. At 8:30 two soldiers appear outside the military food warehouse across the street from me, right next to the metalworkers' yard. The two young men are in different uniforms, representing different branches of the service. They carry guns, but keep them slung over their shoulders for now. Though it is all very relaxed, they keep looking to the east, down the approach road from the barracks. The incessant banging and clanking from the metalworkers' shed fades to a single clink clink clink. Even more eerie is the silence from the road; the thundering truck traffic between Bamako and Dakar has stopped completely. Things are quiet for a while.

Just after 9:00 the gunfire picks up again, this time from the street just behind our house. Single-shot and automatic fire; it's close, and incredibly loud. My heart rate goes up a notch; hmmm, this could be serious. The view is blocked, but I hear muffled shouting in the street: are they protesting the military show of force, or just cussing out idiot soldier-boys for firing off their weapons in the middle of town? Malians – some of them at least – would do that. Good for them. There are no screams (and I'm still thinking it's another army demonstration), so I assume they are firing into the air.

Back on the river-road side there are now about 20 people – adults and kids, including a few women – strung out along the road on both sides of the two soldiers guarding the warehouse across from our house. The air is expectant, subdued, but not obviously fearful. Mr. Camouflage and Mr. Green Fatigues are relaxed and joking with each other. Then suddenly, for no particular reason Camouflage picks up his rifle and fires three shots into the air... and his ammo clip jams. Green fatigues helps him take out the clip and slam it back into the magazine. He fires off seven more shots, some on automatic burst just for show. A woman in the street crowd shouts out *"A manyi!"* (That's bad!) It's the only protest.

No new messages have come in from Peace Corps since the previous day's general warning about avoiding Bamako. I get on the phone and call the other volunteers in town to make sure they are OK. One of them, living in a quiet neighborhood on the edge of Kayes, has heard nothing and is about to hop on a bike and ride across town to her service. Not a good idea, I tell her, what with stray bullets falling from the sky and young boys standing around with rifles and time on their hands. At about 10:30 we all get telephone calls from Peace Corps staff saying that since "the situation is confused," we are being put on Stand-fast alert and quarantine. That translates to "Don't set foot outside your house until further notice, We mean it." At about noon comes a second call from PC, making it official: this is not a demonstration, it's a coup d'état.

So this is the way the world ends, with not a bang but a whimper. It has all been strangely low-key and restrained. No show of heavy weapons, no heroism, no significant resistance or casualties that I am aware of (at least in Kayes); but no joy either. Unlike Moussa Traouré, the dictator who was deposed in 1991, ATT was a genuine statesman and genuinely loved, though it's true that his popularity has faded as the food shortage and Tuareg attacks got worse. His successors? An army Captain and a Lieutenant nobody has ever heard of. The national elections that had been scheduled for next month are now cancelled; it's a whole new ball game. Our village volunteers are saying that their folks accepted it passively – "just another crew of thieves taking over in Bamako" – but Malian lovers of democracy like my friends at the Radio must be disappointed and worried. Their beloved country is facing multiple crises, and has just been commandeered by ambitious beardless boys.

As I write this I am safe enough, but trapped in the house awaiting further orders from Peace Corps, and very much in the dark about what happens next. Asifa called from London to say she is OK, and I'll sleep easier for that tonight. No doubt our friends back home are getting anxious, though, and it would be good to get some kind of message out. So I have asked a colleague at the Radio to swing by and pick up a flash drive with this letter and a list of email addresses. A text just came back with his reply: > *Pray for Mali, pray for Peace.*

Amina.

Postscript Friday, March 23:

Peace Corps has five levels of emergency response. An hour ago we were bumped up to Level Four, *Consolidation*. Orders came down the line to move ourselves, our essential papers, and one suitcase worth of stuff to the nearest Stage House by tomorrow. We are to stay cooped up there for at least another few days and not sortie out to our services, while Peace Corps Mali and Washington figure out what to do. The village volunteers are already making their way toward Kayes. I'm not sure what it all means in the grand scheme of things (maybe nobody does), but if they move to Level Five it means Evacuation. I certainly hope not; I ain't done yet.

March 30, 2012

Consolidated (Zombies optional)

Asifa and I are both doing fine, and are in touch every day via phone and text messages. Ironically, in London she has had even less access to the internet than I have had over the past week, and it's been frustrating for her not being able to write and reassure our friends across the world. If the political weather stays clear, though, all this will soon change: Asifa has got tentative permission from Peace Corps to come back from London this coming Wednesday.

We have both been keeping as busy as circumstances permit: Asifa and some other relatives are helping out with practical arrangements in the wake of her dear aunt's death, while I got special permission to resume my service at the Radio and Community Media Center. Hooray! The bad news is that my house remains off-limits. As we are still on Level Four alert, Consolidation, I have to sleep and spend all non-work time at the Kayes Stage House, which is now brimming with volunteers who have been called in from the outlying villages. No one is allowed outside the courtyard, except to buy food or other essentials.

So life these days feels a lot like crashing in a college dorm over Spring Break, complete with toxic levels of techno-pop on the stereo, mountains of dirty dishes in the sink, and endless hours of conversation comparing the, like, Hotness of boyfriends and reality TV stars. Then there are the water and electricity shutdowns – I'm working on battery at the moment – but I must admit, everyone is trying hard to get along and make it work. And it can't be easy for them; the forced idleness and uncertainty are crazy-making. Day by day the political situation changes, and with it our hopes, bobbing up and down like a yo-yo. Will we see our Malian friends again? Or will the whole cozy Peace Corps family be pulled up and scattered? Then what will I do with my life? I'm not much worried about that last one, but I expect they are.

Mind you, there's been some fun stuff too, like the home-made Zombie movie sent over the internet by a Consolidation group in the south. *One, by one, by one, the trapped, innocent volunteers meet a ghastly fate at the hands of a trusted friend… Pleading, prayers, barricades, even Deep Woods Formula mosquito repellent are of no avail…* What IS it about kids and zombies? I'm so un-hip.

As for the future? Everyone is hopeful, but at this point things are still a bit fluid and uncertain. Consolidation has been extended three times now, and today or tomorrow there will be another announcement after Peace Corps assesses the situation.

What exactly *is* the situation? Many friends have written to say that there's virtually no news about Mali in the media. The short answer is that it's calm, but complicated. Here's a very bare-bones summary of what has been happening:

- Not surprisingly, the coup threw a monkey-wrench into the army's command-and-control structure. The Tuareg separatists have taken advantage of that and taken Kidal, a provincial capital kind of like Kayes but at the east end of the country. Ever cautious, Peace Corps had pulled its volunteers out of Kidal province long before, and none of us were affected. Ironically, the dire military situation is probably the one thing keeping the Malian military unified for the moment.

- There have been a lot of peaceful demonstrations both for and against the coup, but mostly in support of it.

- The junta issued an *Acte Fondamental* (sort of a temporary constitution) suspending the real Constitution and replacing the National Assembly with a council of military and civilian advisors until elections can be held under the auspices of the junta's new regime. Soldiers prevented National Assembly members from entering the parliament building, but they held an emergency session anyway (probably went to Starbucks) and of course declared the whole Acte null and void. Deposed president Amadou Toumani Touré (ATT) turned up alive and well, and says he is willing to resign his office to facilitate a return to democratic governance.

So far so good. But what will convince the coup leaders to back down? Well, for one thing – speaking frankly – the Malian government is on welfare. That's an unkind way of putting it, but the fact is that a large percentage of the central government's operating revenue comes from foreign grants-in-aid. Dunno what the Chinese are doing, but the US and the EU countries have turned off the tap except for humanitarian aid for the food crisis.

More importantly, a couple days ago the Economic Community of West African States (ECOWAS) gave the junta a 72-hour ultimatum: respond positively to the demand for a return to constitutional democracy by Monday April 2, or the Community will impose economic sanctions on Mali. This is the Big Enchilada, and will ultimately have the greatest bearing on whether we'll be able to stay. Mali shares a common currency with several of its neighbors, and they don't want to expose their own economies to the risk of financial chaos if Mali becomes a failed state.

It cuts both ways, of course: the ECOWAS neighbors can *cause* financial chaos in Mali by cutting off transfers from the central bank, effectively putting the whole national economy on a cash basis. That's the threat. Not a pretty prospect, especially if it is combined with embargoes on petrol, cooking gas and other goods. When added to the food shortage such measures could cause serious instability, even for the normally mellow Malians.

Fortunately, it looks more and more like that is not going to happen. News has just come down the pike to the effect that the junta are doing all they can to stave off the ECOWAS sanctions. They have allowed the National Assembly to re-convene in the parliament building, and are negotiating on civilian candidates to head up a transitional government. Best of all, the Peace Corps Country Director just called and said I can travel to Bamako to meet my lady friend if things have settled down enough for her to come back. Yes! It ain't over yet, but maybe soon we can get back to what passes for a normal life around here.

Political Education

It would have been tempting to end with that last paragraph: Let's hear it for the Triumph of Democracy! But that would be doing a disservice to you and to the Malians who took the time to explain their view of events. Read on.

Being sequestered helps keep you safe, but it also prevents you from having real discussions with real people. It wasn't until I was allowed to venture outside the Stage House grounds that I began to get a grassroots political education about the issues surrounding the coup. I had been puzzled by the immediate, easygoing acceptance I saw in the Kayes streets that first day; there were virtually no protests of any kind, and it clearly wasn't because people were being terrorized into submission. Are all Malians really that passive? It turns out they aren't: what I was seeing was *approval* for the coup. Cautious, not passionate or joyous, but approval all the same.

It was the same at the Radio and CMC. After receiving the "Pray for Mali, Pray for Peace" text from a colleague while gunshots were still echoing down the streets, I expected the scene at the Radio to be, well, funereal. After all, these are not fatalistic villagers. They are people who have demonstrated their love for religious tolerance and democracy again and again over the past twenty years, including (among the older guys) being involved in the overthrow of dictator Moussa Traouré in 1991. It's one reason I have felt so comfortable working with them. But there too it was mostly the same mood of cautious approval for the coup, even hope. Why?

Here's a rough composite picture of what they said:

- **Performance:** We are not unhappy about the coup. We never thought of ATT as a bad man; it's just that in the past year or so he has not been an effective President. He made serious mistakes in not supporting our military in the North [i.e. against the Tuaregs], and as a result many soldiers and civilians have been killed. But it's not just that. In the past eight years we have seen no real progress in education or the economy either. No one really holds him responsible for the drought or the food shortage. On the other hand, you can't expect people to be patient when they are hungry.

- **Corruption:** When we were marching for the overthrow of Moussa Traouré, the democrats told us that democracy would make things better. Government would be cleaner, more transparent, more effective. Here we are 21 years later, and corruption is even more widespread and more shamelessly open than in Traouré's time. Corruption is killing this country, and ATT and his people have not done nearly enough to curb it.

- Elections: Yes, we were supposed to have elections in a few weeks, and you can make the case that the coup leaders should not have robbed the people of their right to choose. But in real-world terms you would only be right if (1) we had two or three strong political parties that presented clear choices and would be capable of governing if elected; and (2) we could be sure that the election process would be fair and transparent. What do we have in reality? Forty political parties, each with a splinter of the vote, running every which way like mice. An election process that is controlled by old entrenched interests in Bamako and cannot be trusted.

- Military Government: What do you think we have had for the past eight years, practically speaking? ATT is a former general; all the governors of provinces are former generals, as are half of the cabinet ministers. Civilian versus military is less important than having a constitution that protects human rights, and a government that enforces those protections. Democracy is preferable, but a competent military government can accomplish more real good than a sham democracy. Having said that, we won't continue to support CNRDRE [the junta] if they don't make progress toward transparent elections reasonably soon.

- The International Community: Some people resent the fact that the West threatens to turn off the foreign aid tap if we don't play this the way they want. Foreign governments listen to the politicians in Bamako, who are the very people who have most to gain from keeping arrangements the way they are. I think you will find that the mass of Malians is fed up with the lack of progress, and sympathizes with the objectives of the coup. If the coup Council can succeed in setting the stage for truly fair elections, it will be in Mali's best interest in the long term. Foreigners must try to understand that. You are *born* to democracy, and your democracies work, so you tend to have a blind faith in it. Speaking frankly, blind faith in democracy is not a virtue. It is a blindness.

Strong stuff. It is certainly a dark view of democracy and of politics in general, born of experience. It's equally clear that these are citizens with strong democratic values, despite their support for an action that is anything but democratic. Who was it who said "A cynic is a passionate person who doesn't want to be disappointed again?" Can't say I agree with their choices, but I would invite them into my voting booth anytime.

April 2012, Accra

Evacuation

The letter you just read went out on our very last day of hopefulness. The beardless boys who had seized power refused to step down, and the following day negotiations between the junta and ECOWAS, the West African Economic Community, broke off amid bitter charges of bad faith. A paratroop unit loyal to the old president attempted a counter-coup and went down in flames. Mali's neighbors then resolved to close the borders, in effect throwing the country into economic solitary confinement. Neither money, nor gas, nor anything other than emergency food and medical aid would be allowed in. Even so, Peace Corps Mali was determined to hold on as long as it could, hoping against hope for a change in the political weather. In the PC tradition you do not just cut and run at the first sign of trouble. And in the end we were among the last of the US non-essential personnel to be evacuated.

But the threat of a border closure had introduced a new and sinister dimension to the calculations being made in Bamako and Washington: What would happen if Mali literally ran out of gas? Every spoonful of the country's diesel fuel and petrol has to be trucked across one border or another, and if the gates clanked shut, Mali had as little as two weeks' supply on hand. The Tuaregs and their jihadi allies were making gains day by day, with horrible stories leaking in about Sharia law being imposed at gunpoint in Timbuktu, Mopti and other captured areas. Bamako airport could be closed again at any time on the junta's whim. If worse did come to worst, would our 200-odd scattered volunteers be able to get out at all?

This and many other factors led to the fateful decision. At 6 pm on the evening of April 3 the Kayes volunteers were told, "Pack one bag. You leave from the Stage House at sunup tomorrow morning. We're going to Level Five." Evacuation! The end of 40 years' uninterrupted service in Mali, and the end of all the many projects Asifa and I had planned for the coming year. Over the next eight hours I frantically winnowed our life in Kayes down to two suitcases, one for me and one for the dear girl in London, and fell into bed at exhausted 2:00 am. I hadn't cried in years, but that night I cried myself to sleep. I'M ● NOT ● DONE ● YET!

I locked the doors to our funky old flat and made my way to the Stage House by the dawn's early light. All the Malian staff were there, most with tears in their eyes. Lassine the watchman took my left hand in his left hand and solemnly shook it, in the eloquent Malian gesture that says "This is not goodbye." Troublesome as we surely were, they would miss us. It was some consolation to know that their jobs were secure for now: Peace Corps would keep everyone on the payroll for another at least 12 months or so, in hopes of reviving the program. *Ala ka hɛrɛ fɔ'an kɔ*, my friends. May we leave peace behind us here.

At 6:30 our transport to Bamako showed up, a rattling old Peugeot that was far too small to hold the volunteers and their gear. But it was either that or walk; the official Peace Corps car had already been recalled to Bamako. Lucky for us, West African drivers do not understand the meaning of 'too small,' and after 40 minutes of virtuoso packing and sixteen-clowns-in-a-Volkswagen stuffing ourselves into the seats, we were on our sad way. But not for long: about 60 km out of town the poor overloaded old beast simply lay down and died. It was another two hours before we could find another car (slightly smaller!), but we did eventually make it in to the capital by 11:00 that night.

For the next four days we hunkered down in Tubaniso, the training center outside town. And when I say "we" I mean all 188 of us. It was the first time in PC Mali history that volunteers from all cohorts and regions had been gathered under the same roof, so to speak, and the place just wasn't designed for it. As the Kayes contingent were among the last to arrive, we found ourselves sleeping refugee-style in converted training rooms, ten to twenty beds per room. But hey, we're tough, and there was no whingeing. Just the joy of seeing everybody – including some of the legendary 'site rats' from older stages, who were doing fantastic work but never left their villages – that alone was worth the inconvenience. It was like a wedding and a funeral at the same time. While we caught up with the news and sang by the fire, emptied out our Malian bank accounts and packed parcels to be sent home by ship, the Peace Corps staff were frantically preparing for our next move: five days of close-of-service procedures for a whole country's worth of volunteers. It couldn't be in Mali; it had to be someplace stable.

Togetherness

Officially at least, we volunteers knew neither our destination nor our departure date: all preparations were made as quietly as possible, partly to avoid unnecessary embarrassment to America's friends in Mali, and partly as a security measure. The plane ride was the most vulnerable point in the whole operation, the chance to take out an entire US aid program with a single Stinger missile, if anyone was bent that way. Not likely, of course, but a possibility that had to be reckoned with under the circumstances.

The word came on the morning of Easter Sunday. We assembled our bags and boarded six big buses as our names were read off one by one. Most of the senior staff came too, to help us through the five densely-packed days of paperwork and life choices that lay ahead. Their futures too had taken an abrupt turn in the past two weeks, but they tried not to show it as we crossed the tarmac to the chartered Ethiopian Airlines 737 waiting for final clearance out of Bamako.

Our secret destination? Accra, Ghana. The flight, while not exactly serene, was as uneventful as one could hope for on a plane packed with 200 twenty-somethings decompressing after two weeks of worry and heartache and the forced idleness of consolidation. Some drank, some cried, some told bad jokes way too loudly. Some just sat quietly and stared straight ahead. We zoomed through Ghana Customs in record time, and boarded another fleet of buses to… to THIS?

People ask if I went through culture shock on arriving back in America. The honest answer is No; our five days at the La Palma took care of that. In the larger scheme of things the La Palma is just some three-and-a-half star resort, chosen for the COS conference because it was the only place Peace Corps could find that would accommodate us all on short notice. But for me, that first night in Accra? After 14 months of heat and dust, garbage and khaki-drab, it was a place of unbelievable luxury. Las Vegas on roller skates. My most vivid memory of that first night was the journey to my room in a block of 'chalets' a quarter mile from the reception desk. Here I am, with my bags walking dazedly past an enormous swimming pool, on a broad flagstone path surrounded by flowers and crisp-cut green lawns, sensing faint sounds and smells of the sea… when a liveried bellhop cruises over in a golf cart and insists – in English! – that the spry old gentleman please accept a lift… My room is a suite the size of our whole apartment in Kayes, just for Asifa and me. And most wondrous of all, *everything is clean.* I'm bone-weary and a bit befuddled, and two sentences keep running through my mind like an endless tape loop: "No, it isn't right. I don't deserve this."

Well, that wore off quickly enough; how adaptable we human creatures are. There was just one further luxury that I lacked, and that was delivered at 6:00 the next morning. I heard a knock at the door, and before I knew it a beautiful Indian woman had jumped into my bed! If that isn't five-star service, what is? I hadn't seen Asifa since the night before the coup, when I put her on the bus to Bamako. Peace Corps never did not allow her to return to Mali with the situation so unsettled, but here she was, just a bit tired and bedraggled from the all-night flight from London through Casablanca. After all the craziness it was good to be together again.

The wonders did not cease when we strolled to the poolside restaurant for breakfast. *What is that deliciously sinful smell I smell?* Sweet Jesus; Dead Pigs on a Plate! It was my first taste of pork since leaving America, and thus began the process of transforming me from the lean mean cycling machine of Mali into the decrepit hulk you see before you today.

We feasted like kings those five days at La Palma, but it was also very hard work. The Peace Corps close of service procedures involve much more than signing a few papers and hopping on the plane home. There are seminars on options for employment and post-graduate study, travel arrangements to be made, psychological counseling for those who need it, and endless medical tests. Each volunteer has to create a concise Description of Service that highlights their skills and accomplishments, to help Peace Corps make informed referrals later on.

Things were even more complicated in our case, as it was the biggest evacuation in West African history. Nearly 200 volunteers had to be processed at once, and PC was determined to find new placements around the world for every last one of us who was qualified. An unbelievably complex task. To supplement the Mali staff, Peace Corps flew in a SWAT team of seasoned evacuation specialists, most of them with experience in Africa. American taxpayers take note: These folks worked their tushes off, and did an amazing job. While it's true that they ran us ragged 12 hours a day, we could hardly complain after coming back from an after-dinner pint to see them still hard at work at 11:00 pm.

In the end it paid off. Something like 60 volunteers were sent off to new assignments in Senegal, Cameroun, Belize, Mongolia (!), Fiji, and a dozen other countries. The rest went home – usually after a month or two bumming around the world – to start new lives.

As for us, Ghana was not on the list of countries accepting transfer applications, but in the course of the week Asifa and I had a number of conversations with the #1 and #2 of PC Ghana. There was a big project coming up in the Northern Region, they said, to try out new forms of cooperation between USAID and local government to promote food security. Peace Corps was to be a part of it. The region was a lot like Mali in many respects: dry, Muslim, poor. Work was due to start in the summer, and they needed a couple of experienced hands to develop a training curriculum for the 36 new volunteers who would be assigned to the project. We would come in as Peace Corps Response, not as regular volunteers; Response is a separate division of the organization, which uses experienced volunteers to carry out specific assignments over a specific time period, in this case six to twelve months. Would we be interested?

We sure would. Asifa had family obligations in London, and we both needed a break after 14 months of (almost) vacationless service. We were duly signed, sealed and delivered on April 13 2012, our Mali service officially concluded. After the tearful closing ceremony we went back to pack, and then put on our high-heeled sneakers for a rollicking farewell party that night. *We found love in a hopeless place*... Les Kids played it over and over. It's a silly little song, but I don't doubt that it will make me misty-eyed for many years to come. The next day was a long procession of fond goodbyes: like birds on a branch, in small groups or by the busload, the Mali-*kau* spread their wings and flew.

It had been a hard time for all of us, parting ways with dear friends and colleagues, and grieving for the work left unfinished and the adventures that now would never happen. Saddest of all was the suddenness of it: the way events unfolded gave us hope, right up until the call came to pack that one bag. Then we were wrenched out of our homes and our service literally overnight. I never had a chance to say good-bye, or to tell my Malian friends how grateful I was – I am – for having the chance to know them.

We hung out for a couple days in Accra, sampling the food, eyeing the big sophisticated shops, and getting a feel for the place. Accra was definitely a step above Mali in economic terms, but the people were much more reserved. I sorely missed the armies of little kids shouting Toubab! Toubab! and the Malian way of greeting all who pass you by on the street. Once or twice I forgot myself and called out a hearty Bambara *Ini sɔgɔma!* (good morning) to some innocent soul, only to be met with a confused stare. Well, there will be other chances. Soon we'll be back.

But for now it was time to go; Chicago, San Francisco, Hawaii and London awaited. On the hot, humid night of April 17 we boarded the plane, bound for Ameriki. These days when someone asks where I live, I just smile and say "I live in my shoes."

Postscript

Asifa and I went on to do Peace Corps Response assignments in Ghana and South Africa, finally returning home to Hawaii at the end of 2013. Our Mali comrades scattered to the four corners of the globe, with some taking up new Peace Corps assignments, and others hitting the denim route to see what they could of the world on their way back home. Since then they have made their way up and out into the world as graduate students, entrepreneurs, agriculturalists, health workers, you name it. Not a few have stayed abroad and found a new niche in the NGO world or with the State Department, and some have gone back to Mali. Now and then we hear from them on Facebook.

I also keep in touch with the Radio folks from time to time, and at Radio Rurale de Kayes it seems some of the dreams we dreamed in 2011 finally have come true. These days there is a whole new website, where you can tune in to Kayes music and news and patter from anywhere in the world. -Oh yes; and a web page with the banner "Support your Radio," right next to a long list of financial backers from the Malian Diaspora. Of the CMC folks, Sissoko finally did find his own madonna, and married her. They have produced a bouncing baby boy whom they named... Dauda, of course! Souley also married his sweetheart, though the dream of an internet café of his own still hasn't come true yet. Bintou is finishing a business degree in Kayes, and

I hope that some day she will spread her wings and fly, to experience the wonders of salmon, chalets and whales.

Mali went through some difficult times after April 2012. In the end, the coup didn't help the Malian army one bit; in fact it became even more disorganized. Just a few weeks after we were left, Tuareg rebels took control of all northern and eastern Mali, and declared the independent state of Azawad. Although the Tuaregs are Muslims (like almost everybody else), they are basically nationalists, not jihadi radicals. Still, they joined forces with Al Qaeda in the Islamic Maghreb and a new group calling itself Al Dine. Big mistake! Before long the jihadis took over the cities of Timbuktu, Kidal and Gao, where many volunteers had worked in the past. There they began destroying precious ancient monuments, piously molesting women who weren't dressed according to their standards, and imposing Sharia law on the live-and-let-live Malians at gunpoint.

A turning point came at the beginning of 2013. Having consolidated their gains in the north, the jihadis over-reached themselves and began pushing southwest toward the Malian heartland and Bamako. Things were looking pretty bad for our friends. Then – finally! – the government asked France for help. With strong backing from French paratroop units the Malian army pushed the bad guys back. Asifa and I were in the Philippines at the time, chilling out between our Ghana and South Africa assignments. I remember grisly scenes on the televisions at Cebu airport, and rooting for the French with all my heart.

By the end of January, French troops had taken back all the towns lost in that last awful summer. As they withdrew, a multinational UN force took over in the north, mostly made up of troops from other West African countries. The international community pledged some $4 billion to help rebuild. A few months later Mali held elections, with Ibrahim Keita winning *the presidency. Yeah, he's a Keita, and most assuredly eats beans and donkey when nobody is looking. I can live with that.*

Mali is not out of the woods yet. Though the jihadis have been beaten back for now, the fragile truce with Tuareg rebels broke down in mid-2014. The separatists have taken control of several towns in the north, as negotiations drag on and on. In November Mali's first case of Ebola surfaced in our home town of Kayes. The rains have not been as bad as the disastrous 2011-12 season we witnessed, but the weather is still not back to normal, and may never be.

Still there is much to celebrate. For one thing, 2014 is the 43rd anniversary of the Peace Corps in Mali. The program never did completely shut down, only hibernated. All the Malian staff stayed on payroll for as long as Peace Corps could manage it, and a few key people were kept on to rebuild when the time came. And it has come! In the summer of 2014 a small band of experienced Response volunteers – some of our Kennedys stagemates among them – returned to prepare the way for a grand re-opening in 2015. Already the Facebook scene is buzzing with newbies waiting to embark, breathlessly asking the same questions we asked four years ago: "Do I need to bring a frying pan? Do they have toothpaste? Hey, I found this really cool solar charger that folds up soooooo small….."

And a new story begins.

David Drury
November 2014

Glossary

Al Qaeda in the Islamic Maghreb	A militant Islamic organization that operates in northern Africa and the Sahel region of West Africa. Kidnap for ransom is one of their tactics for raising funds.
APCD	Assistant Peace Corps Director; person in charge of volunteers in a particular line of service, like Health, Education, Agriculture, Small Enterprise Development.
Arab Spring	A revolutionary wave of protests, riots, and civil wars in the Arab world that began in 2010 and led to the overthrow of governments in Libya, Tunisia, and Egypt.
ATT	Malian president Amadou Toumani Touré.
Bamako	Capital of Mali.
basiyirini	Bambara word for Moringa, a tree with edible, nutritious leaves and pods.
bazan	Hand-dyed waxed cotton cloth used to make clothes for ceremonial occasions.
boubou / bubu	A long flowing robe with wide sleeves worn by West African men, especially on formal occasions.
cadeau	Gift; *donne-moi cadeau* is 'Give me a gift.'
campements	Lodgings for travelers in Dogon country.
CFA	Malian money (franc Communauté Financière Africaine); about 500 CFA= $1 US.
CMC	Community media center; internet café without the coffee.

CNRDRE	Military junta formed after the coup of March 2012.
concession	Household compound.
COS	Peace Corps Close of Service procedures.
Coulibaly	David's Malian family name and joking cousins 'clan.' Coulibalys joke with almost everyone.
coups de feu	Gunshots.
Dakar	Capital of Senegal.
Diarra	Asifa's Malian family name and joking cousins 'clan.'
Dogon	An ethnic group living in the central plateau region of Mali, known for its religious traditions, mask dances, wooden sculpture and cliff architecture.
Doromé	An unofficial but widely used unit of money equal to 5 francs CFA.
Dugutigi	Headman or woman of a Bambara village.
ECOWAS	The Economic Community of West African States.
Eid Al-Fitr	Holiday at the end of Ramadan, when people break their fast.
gare	Bus, taxi, or train station.
Griot	A caste of traditional musicians who also act as historians, mediators, and advisors to village leaders.
Homestay	Living in a village during Peace Corps basic training.
IST	Peace Corps in-service training.
Insha'Allah	God willing.

jihadi / jihadist	Proponent of religious 'holy war.'
joking cousins	Relationship between certain ethnic or family-name groups, where they treat each other like cousins or close family, especially to exchange humorous insults.
Keita	One of the joking cousins 'clans;' a joking arch-enemy of David's clan, the Coulibalys.
LCF	Peace Corps Language and Cultural Facilitator.
Kennedys	The name given to David and Asifa's *stage* or training cohort. -Not to be confused with Team America, Risky Business, the Mad Hatters, or the Goodfellas.
Les Kids	The young Peace Corps volunteers.
Mango rains	Pre-monsoon showers that usually start in April.
Matrone	Midwife; responsible for women and children's primary health care.
mɔni	Porridge or gruel made from millet.
moto	Motorcycle.
Moussa Traoré	President/ dictator of Mali from 1968 to 1991.
NGO	Non-governmental agency or non-profit organization, such as the UN, CARE, Oxfam, Médecins sans Frontières, or Peace Corps.
ɲɛgɛn	Outhouse; latrine.
pagne	An untailored cotton cloth used as a wrap-around skirt or head tie, among other things.
PCV	Peace Corps volunteer.

Peace Corps Partnership program	A funding source for small projects initiated by volunteers; operates a little like Kickstarter.
pinasse	Wooden river boat with a small motor.
Ramadan	Muslim month of fasting.
refectoire	Dining hall.
RRK	Radio Rurale de Kayes.
Sahel	Semi-arid zone of transition in Africa, between the Sahara Desert and wetter savanna lands to the south.
salidaga	Bucket or teapot-shaped water vessel for washing the hands.
service	A volunteer's main job or assignment.
Sharia law	Islamic religious law based on interpretations of the Koran and the words and actions of the prophet Muhammad.
stage	Cohort of Peace Corps volunteers trained at the same time.
Stage House	Peace Corps regional transit house, where volunteers can stay when away from their home villages.
stagiaire	Trainee; term used for Peace volunteers during pre-service training.
Tabaski	Big Muslim feast celebrated 40 days after Eid Al-Fitr and the end of Ramadan. Also called Eid al-Adha. Honors Abraham's willingness to sacrifice his son Ishmael at God's command.
Toubab / Toubabu	White person; foreigner.

Touregs	A Berber people from the desert North of Mali.
Tubaniso	Peace Corps training center outside Bamako (literally "Home of the Dove").
tunkeranke	The Malian Diaspora; Malian migrants living abroad.
UNESCO	United Nations Educational, Scientific and Cultural Organization.
USAID	United States Agency for International Development.
Wolof	Language used in Senegal, Gambia, and parts of Mali.

About the Authors

Asifa Kanji grew up in Tanzania and Kenya, was schooled in England, fell in love and followed her heart to America in 1975. She has been a teacher, a henna artist, a computer programmer, a dilettante, a care giver and a traveler who loves to write. When she is not someplace else, she lives in Hawaii or Oregon with her editor, her publisher, her chief art critic, and her husband.

David Drury has been a university Lecturer, an applied social science researcher in the US and a bunch of other countries, a truck driver, Census taker, and London busker. David lives in Hilo or Ashland with his Most Difficult Client, and strives to achieve moderation in all things, including moderation.

Made in the USA
San Bernardino, CA
07 May 2015